STORIES FROM ASIA TODAY

S0-CUD-249

Stories from Asia Today

A Collection for Young Readers

Book Two

sponsored by the
Asian Cultural Centre for Unesco

New York · WEATHERHILL / HEIBONSHA · *Tokyo*

RENNER LEARNING RESOURCE CENTER
ELGIN COMMUNITY COLLEGE
ELGIN, ILLINOIS 60120

808.83
1884

This is the second volume of Asian contemporary stories to be published under the Asian Copublication Programme carried out, in cooperation with Unesco, by the Asian Cultural Centre for Unesco / Tokyo Book Development Centre. The stories have been selected and, with the editorial help of the publishers, edited by a five-country central editorial board in consultation with the Unesco member states in Asia.

First edition, 1980

Jointly published by John Weatherhill, Inc., of New York and Tokyo, with editorial offices at 7–6–13 Roppongi, Minato-ku, Tokyo 106, Japan; and Heibonsha, Tokyo. Copyright © 1980 by the Asian Cultural Centre for Unesco / Tokyo Book Development Centre, 6 Fukuro-machi, Shinjuku-ku, Tokyo 162. Printed in Japan.

LIBRARY OF CONGRESS CATALOGING IN PUBLICATION DATA: Main entry under title: Stories from Asia today / (Asian copublication programme series four: book 1–2) / "Sponsored by Asian Cultural Centre for Unesco" / SUMMARY: A collection of contemporary short stories from 15 Asian countries. / 1. Children's stories, Oriental—Translation into English / 2. Children's stories, English—Translation from Oriental languages / [1. Asia—Fiction. 2. Short stories] / I. Asian Cultural Centre for Unesco / PZ5.S8819 / 1979 / 808.83′1 / 79–19059 / ISBN 0–8348–1040–9 (v. 2)

064421

Contents

BANGLADESH

A New School for Anu

by Syed Shamsul Hoque

Early in the morning Anu got up and took his bath. This was the day his father was going to enter him in a new school.

He felt very happy. His father had been transferred to this city very recently, and Anu had not yet had time to make any friends. He was lonely. It was not studies that he missed but the chance to make friends. He was anxious to begin school.

Several times he came and asked his mother if breakfast was not ready yet. "Please, Mother, give me my breakfast. Why, it's almost ten o'clock."

"It's nothing of the sort," his mother said with some annoyance, rapidly stirring a pot that was simmering on the stove.

"That's all you know about it," said Anu in a low voice, pouting. "I'm sure to be late for school." He leaned impatiently against the kitchen door.

His elder sister was slicing some raw vegetables. She looked up and said: "It's only eight-thirty now, Anu. I've never seen you in such a hurry to go to school." Laughing, she began slicing vegetables again.

Not wanting to tell them his real reason for wanting to get to school, he pretended to be angry and said to his sister: "Am I supposed to be lazy like you and just sit home all day? Don't I have to go to school and study hard?"

His mother laughed and said to his sister: "Just see what a serious little scholar our Anu has become."

"Oh, yes," his sister said with a sly smile, "he's told me that he wants to be a railway guard. Maybe that's the reason he must study so hard."

"Aw, what do you know about it anyway?" Anu cried. "She's lying, Mother, I never told her any such thing."

He ran out of the kitchen, thinking angrily: She really doesn't have any sense at all. Why must she tell Mother everything? Wasn't it a secret, what I told her? I honestly can't stand Sister sometimes. She's always blabbing secrets. All right, so maybe I want to be a guard, but what's that to her? The railway people would hardly make a guard out of any Tom, Dick, or Harry. What does she know about how much courage, and intelligence, and study it takes to become a railway guard?

Honestly, he went on thinking to himself, it might not be such a bad idea if I could become a guard. Just think how many distant cities I could see. And what fun the job would be! Red and green flags in my hands, a whistle in my mouth, a pair of white trousers and a jacket with brass buttons and flaps over the pockets, and on my head a cap with a shiny back visor. The driver may run the engine, but he can't start the train moving unless the guard blows his whistle. And he has to stop if the guard waves his red flag. Yes, sir, a guard's job is no joke.

Suddenly Anu felt unhappy. He wouldn't be grown up for a long time; it would be ten or twenty years anyway before he could become a railway guard. In the meantime there was nothing he could do but wait. He would simply have to put up with their jokes, their teasing smiles.

He went out of the house and stood by the side of the street, watching the passing crowd. Bullock carts were on the way to the bazaar, their rusty wheels creaking. A bus came from the opposite way, going toward the railway station. That meant it was already nine o'clock: the Ulipur bus,

9

jammed with passengers, passed their house every day at nine.

He hurried back inside the house, but he could not gather up enough courage to go into the kitchen and ask his mother for breakfast again. Somehow, suddenly he was overcome with a strange shyness, and yet he was as anxious as ever to rush to his new school this very minute and take his seat among his new friends-to-be.

Going to his room, he opened a small suitcase and took out a pair of freshly laundered shorts and a new shirt. His father had bought the shirt for him only last week—one with blue stripes and a paper label still stuck on the collar. He tore off the label and put the shirt on. The smell of new clothing still clung to it. How pleasant! And how smooth the new cloth felt against his skin!

Just then his sister called him to breakfast. Taking his seat at the table, Anu saw that his mother had taken particular care with the food today, and he was being given special treatment. His mother took out a new plate for him, one with

10

a beautiful flowered pattern. This was to celebrate his going to a new school.

When the rice was heaped on his plate, he could feel the warmth of its steam rising to his face. A sweet smell filled his nostrils. His sister poured a spoonful of the melted butter called ghee over his rice, and his mother served him some mashed potatoes. But everything was too hot to eat. His mother fanned the food a bit with an edge of her blouse, and Anu blew on it. Then he mixed the potatoes with the rice and took a mouthful. It was as delicious as honey.

His sister said: "Don't be in a rush, Anu. There's plenty of time. Eat your fill."

"Don't worry," said Anu, "I will." But after he began eating he discovered that he was not hungry at all. He found that he could hardly swallow a bite.

His sister went on: "If you don't have a good breakfast now, when you meet the headmaster fear will fill your empty belly and you won't be able to say a word."

"Oh, no," said Anu, "there's nothing to be afraid of."

"He'll ask you questions to see how much you know. Will you be able to answer?"

"Of course I will. Let him ask as many questions as he wants. I'll be able to answer them, all right."

Anu's mother beamed. She looked first at her son and then at her daughter. "My Anu is really a good student," she said.

His sister gave him a delicious helping of padba fish cooked with sliced onions. It was a golden color and was still steaming. The very sight made Anu's mouth water. He picked up his glass of water and drank it in gulps.

He was just about to begin on the fish when they heard his father calling from outside. He had gone to his office early that morning, promising to come back at ten o'clock to get Anu and take him to school. And now here he was.

His sister went out and said: "Anu's still eating breakfast, Father."

Anu heard his father reply: "Well, tell him to get moving. I have to hurry back to the office after taking him to school."

And not another mouthful could Anu swallow. He felt his heart beating fast. An unknown fear gripped him. He felt dizzy. He got up and started washing his face and hands.

His mother cried: "Why, Anu, you can't be finished yet."

"Yes, Mother, I've had enough."

He ran outside for a minute and saw his father waiting on his bicycle. Then he ran back to his room, dried his face and hands, grabbed up his school books, and, with a last quick look in the mirror, ran back out to his father. His mother stood watching from the front door.

His father said: "You look nice in your new shirt. Did you have plenty to eat?"

"Yes."

"Well, aren't you going to touch your mother's feet and ask her blessings?"

Anu felt embarrassed. Did he really have to go through all the foot-touching ceremony just because he was entering a new school? Caught in this dilemma, he stood motionless.

His mother came to his rescue. She drew her son to her, stroked his head, and said: "Pay good attention to your studies, my son, and don't get into any trouble. Do you promise?"

Anu nodded in assent. He jumped onto the bar of the bicycle in front of his father, and his father pedaled away. Glancing back, Anu saw his mother and sister looking after them, smiling fondly. . . .

Two long classrooms and a small office or two—that's all there was to Mohimpur Elementary School for Boys. In front there was a large open space covered with patches of green grass, at each end of which there stood a goal post blackened by sun and rain. Several different kinds of tropical trees spread their branches over the school building, all but hiding its roof with their dense clusters of leaves. The corrugated iron sheets of the roof were thickly covered with moss.

Anu gaped at the sight, his mouth hanging open. So this was his new school!

Classes had already started. Through the large windows he could see rows of heads. Some of the boys were reading books, some were writing, some were just staring into space, and some were whispering among themselves when they could avoid the teacher's eye.

Reaching the playing field, Anu and his father got off the

bicycle. As they walked on toward the school, his father said: "How about arithmetic? Do you remember how to do your sums?"

Anu answered yes by bending his head to one side. His father leaned the bicycle against the wall and entered the headmaster's office, with Anu following him.

Inside the office, Anu saluted the headmaster and stood looking at him with frightened eyes. For a moment all he could see was the man's bald head, sunken cheeks, a pair of bright eyes, and a greasy jacket. Anu was still more frightened, and it seemed as if the man, who looked so angry and grave, would start shouting at any moment.

Gradully Anu turned his frightened eyes to look slowly around the room. A world map hung on the wall. Through the dusty glass panes of a cabinet he could see neatly arranged books and registers; two of the panes had been broken and patched up with cardboard. There was a long table on one side of the room flanked by a few chairs. On the table lay a blackboard eraser, some sticks of chalk, and a cane made from a slender branch of a tamarind tree. The cane looked sleek and flexible. Were bad students switched with this? Oh, how it must hurt!

"Come here, my boy." The headmaster's booming voice startled Anu. He took a few slow, timid steps until he was in front of the headmaster's desk. Glancing back, he saw his father smiling encouragingly at him. He could barely make out what it was his father was saying to the headmaster. He began to sweat. My god, was it English they were talking in? Was he going to be examined in English?

Turning to Anu, the headmaster spoke carefully, slowly: "What is your name?"

"My name is Anwar Hossain. I am the son of Moulavi Gholam Hossain."

"Very good."

14

Suddenly Anu felt light as a feather. No, he hadn't made a single mistake. He heard his father saying that he himself helped Anu with his studies every day in the morning and evening.

"I was transferred here rather suddenly," his father went on. "Unless he starts school again now, he'll begin forgetting what he's learned. He was in the fourth grade at his former school."

All of a sudden the headmaster turned to Anu and said: "If a maund of rice costs thirty-five taka, how much do eight seer of rice cost?"

Anu began to mutter and to search his memory of arithmetic. What was that general rule now? But no matter how hard he tried, he simply could not remember. He began to tremble, and his throat felt dry, but he could not remember the rule. He stood there silently, his head bowed. Once he glanced at his father and saw his father's eyes on him.

The headmaster repeated the question. But still Anu could not answer and began scratching the floor with the nail of his big toe.

His father laughed and said: "He's always been a little weak in arithmetic." Then he turned to Anu and said: "If a maund costs thirty-five taka, then what is the price of one seer? Then all you need do is multiply that by eight and you have the price of eight seer, right?"

Anu swallowed and said, hesitantly: "The price of one seer?"

"Yes."

"Oh, let it go," said the headmaster, coming to Anu's rescue. Then he picked up a book, selected a poem in it, and asked Anu to read it aloud.

Freed from the arithmetic problem, Anu tried to make up for his failure and began to read very carefully in a resonant voice. It was Dwijendra Lan Roy's beautiful poem in

15

Bengali which so movingly expresses love for the land of Bengal, or Bangladesh as the country is now called.

After Anu had feelingly recited a few lines the headmaster raised a hand and said: "All right, that will do."

Glancing back, Anu could see that his father was pleased with him. He saw with surprise that his father's eyes were glistening with tears. Their pupils look brighter, bigger, and darker than usual. Strongly moved, Anu closed the book, clutched it to his breast, and stood motionless.

The headmaster looked at him and said: "What is the meaning of the phrase 'horit kshetra?' "

"Horit kshetra?" Again Anu was in difficulty. He did not know the meaning of the word "horit." Mentally, he repeated to himself the line of the poem that contained these words. He knew what "kshetra" meant; it was a field. So what would "horit kshetra" be? Then he suddenly remembered the next line of the poem, in which the word "paddy" was used. He quickly said: " 'Horit kshetra' means 'paddy field.' "

Immediately the smile left his father's face, and Anu realized his answer was wrong. He lowered his head.

But the headmaster consoled him, saying: "Well, your answer is partly correct. 'Horit' means green, and a paddy field is also green. So 'horit kshetra' means 'green field.' Whenever you come across a new word whose meaning you do not know, ask you father or your teacher and find out its meaning. And then repeat the meaning a few times until you've memorized it. Do you understand?"

"Yes, sir."

"Also write the spelling of the word ten times in your exercise book and learn it thoroughly."

Anu inclined his head to one side, indicating that he would do so.

The headmaster took the book of poems from Anu and, turning to his father, said: "All right, let Anwar Hossain join

16

the fourth-grade class now. We'll see later how he's come along. He seems to be quite a smart lad."

Anu realized that words of praise were being said about him. He felt shy and embarrassed. He ought to have been able to do the arithmetic problem. And all of a sudden he remembered the method. That was it: if a maund of rice cost thirty-five taka, the price of a seer would be fourteen anna, and, well, the price of eight seer would be seven taka. Now he knew the answer, but he could not bring himself to say it aloud. Shyly, he looked around. Should he just go ahead and blurt it out? No, now it was too late. Oh, how hard he had tried earlier, but he simply couldn't remember the method. He was not really weak in arithmetic. His father was wrong about that. Well, as soon as they were back home he would

tell his father that the price of eight seer of rice was exactly seven taka.

Suddenly the headmaster called out in a loud voice: "Biltu, Biltu."

The school porter hurried into the room. So Biltu was the name of the porter instead of a new problem. That was funny.

The headmaster said to the porter: "Take the boy to the fourth grade."

Anu felt rather sad at the thought of parting from his father, who was getting ready to leave. His father stopped near the door and said: "Can you get home by yourself after school or shall I send Yasin for you?"

Anu vigorously moved his head sidewise. No, no, he could go home by himself.

The porter walked away with long strides, and Anu found it difficult to keep up. After taking a few steps he looked back and saw that his father was still standing where he had left him, in just the same way that his mother and sister had stood looking after him when he had left for school. His father's eyes looked very bright. Anu suddenly told himself that he could very well have touched his mother's feet and asked her blessings before he left home. He regretted the omission. "But," he said to himself, "I promise to study hard, Mother, and not to get in any trouble."

As he stepped into the classroom, Anu looked back once more and saw his father smiling at him. He smiled back.

Then he followed the porter up to the teacher's desk.

Translated by Kabir Chowdhry
Illustrated by Hashem Khan

BURMA

The Soccer Game

by Gayetni

Editors' Note. Soccer, sometimes called association football, is one of the three main types of football, the other two being rugby and American football, and is very popular in many parts of the world. It differs from the other football games principally in that the players are almost never allowed to touch the ball with their hands but only to kick it or hit it with other parts of the body.

Win Mg is in high spirits as he waits for the beginning of the soccer match his team is to play against Kaingdan Primary School. Looking around at his teammates, he feels quite satisfied. He's a forward player, and he knows that the players on his team have confidence in his abilities.

In the match against Shwe Kanyinbin Primary School his

team won with a score of three to one. That was quite a victory for Win Mg's team, and Win Mg himself had shot two of the goals. Also, in their match with Tawlay Village, they had won by a score of two to zero, one of the goals being made by Win Mg.

Now the eastern skies are black with rain clouds. It's going to rain hard soon, but the team hasn't arrived yet. On each side of the field the fans are restless. They have come from all the neighboring villages—paddy farmers, planters, cowherds, monastery schoolboys, shop owners—it's quite a large and varied crowd.

The goals are made of bamboo posts, standing tall and straight at each end of the field, holding nets between them. The ground is a sandy soil that gives the players a good grip for their feet while running.

"Here they come!" someone shouts from the crowd.

The other team and a number of other people can be seen coming out of the gates of Kaingdan Village, walking slowly and leisurely. Their coach, who is already on the field, turns to Win Mg and says: "Well, are you ready to play? Do you think you can beat us?"

"We're going to do our best to win," answers Win Mg. "We've been training hard."

By this time the Kaingdan team has reached the field, just at the appointed time. Win Mg's team had arrived a little early. The referee, a high school student from a nearby town, walks toward the center of the field, and the audience comes to life with wild shouts.

Both teams walk toward midfield. The captains of the teams toss a coin while the referee watches. The Kaingdan team gains the southern end of the field, and Win Mg's team has the northern.

The referee whistles to signal the start of play. Tun Khin boots the ball to Win Mg. Win Mg dribbles the ball and passes it on to Hla Kywe. The opponents tackle them. Both sides are fighting hard to gain the ball, which rolls to and fro around midfield.

Once the ball touches someone's hand on Win Mg's side and they are penalized. They have to make a big effort to avoid being scored against.

Then the ball crosses over the center line to the Kaingdan side. Hla Kywe dodges one after another of the opposing players and carries the ball forward. Win Mg runs ahead, anticipating that the ball will be passed to him.

Hla Kywe dodges yet another opponent and pretends that he is going to try to shoot a goal. But then suddenly he kicks the ball to Win Mg, and the other side is caught off guard by this surprise move. Win Mg connects with the ball and in a hard shot bangs it toward the goal. The goalkeeper of the other side makes a dive but fails to stop the ball.

"Goal!" shouts the audience.

Hla Kywe and Ko Than run to hug Win Mg, who is feeling quite proud of his goal.

Play goes on. Whenever the ball gets to Win Mg's feet the whole audience roars to encourage him.

"Hooray for Win Mg!"

"Do you best, Win Mg!"

Win Mg hears these shouts of encouragement even while he chases the ball around the field. He feels quite satisfied with himself and resolves to try still harder so everyone will really know how good he is.

The first half ends with a score of one to zero in favor of Win Mg's side. During the five-minute interval, Win Mg struts around the field, feeling more and more pleased with himself.

"We're going to win for sure," Win Mg tells the young teacher who is the coach of his team.

"And that will make us the champions in this region," answered the teacher. "So do your best, boys."

The referee walks to midfield and blows his whistle. The players take their positions, having switched ends of the field. And the second half begins with another blast of the whistle.

Win Mg's side, one goal ahead, keeps pressing its opponents. Win Mg can think of nothing but showing how good he is. So he begins to concentrate upon individual play.

Whenever the ball comes to him, he doesn't pass it on to anyone else but races toward the goal alone. He is constantly trying to make goals by himself.

Meanwhile the Kaingdan team scores a goal. This makes Win Mg angry and he runs about the field still harder.

At one point Win Mg is dribbling. If he passes the ball to Hla Kywe, who is ready to receive it, there's a good chance for a goal. But he doesn't pass the ball. And while he's dribbling alone, an opposing player takes possession of the ball.

"Hey, Win Mg," Hla Kywe calls in an angry voice, "why didn't you pass to me?"

But Win Mg doesn't answer. All he can think about is how he'll shoot a goal himself soon.

The game becomes still more furious, and the Kaingdan team scores again.

Win Mg's face turns red, and he runs after the ball with all his might. But his efforts come to nothing, and soon the referee's whistle ends the game. The score is two to one in the Kaingdan team's favor. Win Mg's side has lost.

RENNER LEARNING RESOURCE CENTER
ELGIN COMMUNITY COLLEGE
ELGIN, ILLINOIS 60120

On the way back home Win Mg walks with his head hanging down. He can no longer boast that he's the champion.

The goalie walks beside him and berates him: "It's just because you played all by yourself. Do you realize we lost just because you wouldn't pass the ball to anyone else? You played to please yourself because you know everyone thinks you're the best, didn't you?"

At these words Win Mg suddenly realizes his mistake. He'd ignored the ability of his teammates and thought too much only of himself. He had simply forgotten that a team's collective strength is bigger than the strength of any one player. He'd been so proud of his own skill that he'd forgotten everything else. Now he can see that, despite their winning start, his team had lost because of him.

He went on thinking to himself: It really is my fault. We've lost because I thought so highly of myself. I'm to blame for our losing. If only I'd played the usual team game, we'd have won. Even my initial goal was thanks to Hla Kywe's pass.

I was the only one who didn't have confidence in the others. The rest had confidence in one another and played with team spirit. Shame on me!

Win Mg feels more and more bitter. He cannot forgive himself.

"Yes, my friends," he says aloud to the teammates around him, "it's all my fault. I'm to blame for our losing. It's because I was too proud of myself. Because I didn't have confidence in all of you. I did the wrong thing."

Thus does Win Mg admit his fault, feeling very, very sorry as he and his teammates walk on toward home.

Translated by San Lwin
Illustrated by Myo Win

Beside the Sea

by Xiao Ping

How glad Second Lock was to be visiting his grandmother's again! It was over five years since he had been here.

Granny lived by the sea. North of the village was an estuary where a stream entered the sea. At high tide it was one huge sheet of water—there seemed no end to it; but at low tide a stretch of golden sand appeared on either side. South of the village were sand dunes covered with knotgrass, and it was from these dunes that he could see the open waters of the Yellow Sea. He loved to gaze at the sea, a vast expanse of sapphire blue with golden flecks dancing over it. There were fish, crabs, and lobsters in it. There must be some very big fish too. His teacher had told him that some sea creatures were bigger than houses, but Second Lock had never seen such fish. As a matter of fact, he hadn't seen so much as a small one since coming here. He wondered where they'd all gone.

With Granny lived Second Lock's uncle and aunt, their son Tiger, and their daughter Petal. Second Lock played on the beach every day with Tiger. The sand was fine and soft. They lay on their backs, unbuttoned their shirts, and basked in the sun. Tiger was a year older than Second Lock, but not as tall; and since they were both in the fourth grade, Second Lock didn't think much of him. True, he was a squad leader in the Young Pioneers; but Second Lock had become a Young Pioneer himself just before the holidays, and he thought his own squad leader far more capable than Tiger.

On the other hand, as Second Lock finally had to admit, Tiger knew much more about the sea than he did. He knew, for instance, just when the tide would turn, what kind of tide brought fish with it, and what kind of weather brought the crabs out. But Second Lock couldn't understand why his cousin always had to be making fun of him because he didn't know much about the sea.

"Granny," he once said, "I saw sails today. Snow white they were. Ever so many of them. Far out to sea, and they weren't moving at all."

"Not moving?" put in Tiger. "How do you know they weren't moving? It's just that they were far away and you couldn't see, that's all."

Another time, Second Lock picked up some pretty, boat-shaped objects on the beach and showed them to Tiger with delight.

"They're just cuttlebones," Tiger said with a snort. "We throw them away, but here you are bringing them home."

And Petal ran to tell her grandmother: "Granny, Second Lock has been bringing cuttlebones home."

Why couldn't the little busybody hold her tongue?

Second Lock liked to squat on the beach beyond the dunes when the tide came in, watching the waves rolling in from the distant horizon. When the roaring, foaming water seemed about to engulf him, he would jump backward. Then the waves receded just as they reached his feet, and cool salt water sprayed over his face. The next moment the tide would be after him again, and he'd have to jump farther back. In this way, he fancied, he could lead the sea right up to the foot of the dunes. But when he climbed one of the dunes, instead of following him, the sea gradually calmed down. Second Lock was disappointed. He had hoped to lure it right up over the dunes.

What Second Lock enjoyed most was fishing with Tiger. Once they took Uncle's fishing net without telling him, and ran to the estuary. The tide was rolling in.

"Quick, Second Lock!" Tiger called softly, pointing at the water. "Look at that shoal of fish."

Not a single fish could Second Lock see. But from that moment Tiger seemed a grown-up in his eyes. He believed his cousin's every word and unhesitatingly did everything he said. Sure enough, while they were still drawing the net ashore, Second Lock saw fish leaping and struggling in it. Anxious and overjoyed, he grew hoarse from shouting. This one catch filled half a bucket. Second Lock stared at the fish and could hardly believe his eyes.

When the tide was out, he and Tiger would dig clams from the beach beside the estuary. The clams that Tiger found were as big as Second Lock's fist, with thick, beautifully marked shells; but they buried themselves so deep in the sand and the tide had always washed the beach so smooth that Second Lock could not find a single one, however hard he looked. Each time Tiger used his hoe, though, he unearthed one. Then Tiger explained that there was a tiny hole over each clam's hiding place because it needed air, and Second Lock saw such holes all along the beach. Still, when he dug them up the only clams he found were no larger than his thumb. He was very disappointed. At that, Tiger told him that most of the clams on that part of the beach had already been taken, but there were plenty left on the far shore of the estuary, and if Second Lock liked, maybe they would go there to dig for them someday.

Second Lock was too pleased for words! He longed to take a big box full of clams home with him. Then when school began he would spread five, ten, or even more clamshells on his desk, to the envy of his classmates. One shell would hold slate pencils, one ink, one red paint, another green. . . . His schoolfellows were bound to gather round for a look, and he'd give them one shell each. No, on second thought, he'd only give shells to his friends, not to those he didn't like.

But while he looked forward to being taken to the other side of the estuary, his cousin seemed to have forgotten all about it. And pride prevented Second Lock from asking for any favor, much as he longed to go.

It was dusk one day when Second Lock and Tiger came back from the beach. Aunty and Granny were preparing supper, with Petal tagging after them and begging to see what they were making. Once when Granny turned round, she nearly knocked the little girl over.

"How do you expect me to get anything done?" she snapped. "I seem to have grown a tail."

Petal seized the hem of her jacket. "What are you making?" she asked. "Please let me see."

"Be a good girl now, Petal," said Granny, holding a stack of bowls in her hands. "Go and play with Second Lock."

"I don't want to," Petal pouted.

"You don't want to. Huh!" thought Second Lock. "I wouldn't play with you even if you begged me."

After supper, Granny and Aunty washed up while Tiger fed the pigs and then swept the courtyard. Second Lock got ready for sleep by spreading a mat on the threshing floor in front of the house and lying down on it. The sky glittered with stars. From time to time a cool, salty breeze blew in from the sea. He couldn't sleep, partly because of the mosquitoes buzzing round him and partly because he was wishing so hard to catch those clams Tiger had told him about.

Soon Tiger came out with another mat under his arm. He spread this beside Second Lock and, lying down, whispered: "Let's dig for clams on the far shore of the estuary tomorrow. Are you game? Or don't you dare?"

"Of course I dare!" cried Second Lock, springing to his feet. "Why should I be afraid?"

"Don't shout." warned Tiger, punching him in the leg. "We mustn't let Dad know."

33

Second Lock opened his eyes wide. "Why not?" he whispered.

"Why not? Children aren't allowed to go north of the estuary. You can get drowned there at high tide if you don't run very fast."

"Then what should we do?" Second Lock felt a little scared.

"It's all right. We'll start back as soon as the tide starts coming in."

Uncle came to the gate with a shirt thrown over his shoulders and sent Tiger off with a message to the co-op. Second Lock was excited and started imagining all sorts of fascinating things before he dozed off. That night he had many dreams. He and Tiger were digging up a whole basketful of clams. The basket became so heavy they couldn't lift it, and while they were struggling with it the tide bore down on them like a moving wall. He started crying with terror, while Tiger swam away. The tide drew nearer and nearer and as he turned and raced toward the beach another great wave barred his way. He jumped and woke up in a cold sweat, his heart drumming wildly. The red sun was rising over an island in the sea, and the threshing floor was deserted.

Second Lock got up and ran into the house with the mat under his arm. Aunty was carrying rice to the table, Tiger was feeding pigs in the courtyard, and Granny was telling Petal a story. As soon as they sat down to eat, Second Lock started shoveling rice into his mouth as if he were pouring it down his throat. Granny watched him in dismay and set down her bowl.

"Don't bolt your food like that, Second Lock," she scolded.

Petal craned her neck to see what her cousin was doing, but he had already finished.

He slipped to the gate of the courtyard and waited there impatiently for Tiger. After what seemed an age his cousin

appeared. They winked at each other and set off at a run toward the sea.

"Tiger," Uncle suddenly called after them. "Where are you taking your cousin? You haven't even swept the courtyard yet."

Tiger came to a sudden stop, like a car abruptly braking. Second Lock's heart sank, but Granny came to their rescue.

"Let the boys go," she said to Uncle. "They've been hard at their books for a whole year. Let them do as they like for a change. 'Even the devil needs a holiday.' "

Then Uncle relented, simply warning them: "All right, but remember you mustn't cross the estuary."

Tiger shouted something in reply. Then he took Second Lock's hand, and the two went running on.

The tide was at low ebb. The sky was azure blue, and the sun on the golden sand dazzled their eyes. Tiny crabs were busily digging holes. They had dotted the smooth beach with balls of sand like peas and were still throwing more and more up. The thrown sand glistened in the sunshine like pearls and whirled in the air for a second before falling to the ground. A warm breeze was blowing, bringing with it the tang of the ocean.

"Oh, no!" Tiger stopped. "We forgot the basket and hoe."

Second Lock halted too. Tiger looked back and then cast a glance at the sun. "Never mind," he said, waving his hand with a gesture of dismissal. "Let's go on. We can scoop them up with our hands and wrap them in our shirts."

They ran on again. The soft sand balls crackled beneath them, pleasantly tickling the soles of their bare feet, and soon they came to a line of jagged rocks. These rocks were not very tall, and at high tide they would become a reef with only their tops showing above water.

"This must be it," thought Second Lock.

Looking back, he found that Granny's house had disappeared. Ahead, in the estuary, a narrow white strip of water was still gleaming faintly, just as before, when he had looked across from the shore. "Aren't we nearly there?" he asked.

"We've still quite a way to go." Tiger did not even look up. "We've only come one mile out of three."

"What! Three miles? Won't that take us right into the sea?"

But Tiger raced forward without a word. And, not wanting to seem a coward, Second Lock followed.

After crossing the sand, they came to a mud flat. The mud was sticky and slippery and was embedded with sharp stones and broken shells. Second Lock cut his feet time and again and found it harder and harder to walk the farther they went. He picked his way carefully on tiptoe but had to pull his feet out after every step. Even so, he stumbled several times, till his white shirt and trousers were smeared with mud, and

36

his backside ached from falling. Not once, though, did Tiger fall. He pattered on, bringing his soles down flat on the mud, and stopped every so often for his cousin.

The sun was almost directly overhead by the time they reached the estuary. What had seemed a white thread from afar was actually broad enough to carry a large junk. Tiger calmly stripped off his clothes and, holding them in one hand high above his head, waded slowly into the water; Second Lock followed suit, keeping close behind him. The tide was ebbing very swiftly. Second Lock could barely keep his balance and nearly fell again. Fortunately the water was not deep, reaching only to their armpits. Tiger supported his cousin with one hand until they reached the far shore.

They were now on a vast golden beach. It stretched as far as the eye could see, and not a soul was in sight. Tiger put down his clothes and set to work building two sand castles at the water's edge. Second Lock was wondering what his cousin was doing when Tiger stood up and said: "I'm going farther on, where there are lots of clams. But you must stay here to keep watch. Call me when the tide turns and begins to wash these castles away. Then we'll have to start back at once."

Second Lock was not too pleased with this arrangement, but he had to agree to it.

Tiger ran on, naked as he was. Second Lock lay on the beach and fixed his gaze on the sand castles. The sun beat down on him, and soon a gauze-like layer of white salt covered his body. Beginning to feel lonely, he sat up and looked around. Tiger was far away. In the distance, some sea gulls were circling low over the ocean. All at once he felt quite deserted and began to panic. There was no one near. He couldn't even see his grandmother's house. What would he do if the tide came in suddenly? His flesh began to creep and he glanced around nervously.

37

He remembered an accident that had happened at home the previous summer. It was a fine day and he was bathing with some classmates in the river near his village. The water was clear, and not too deep. But all of a sudden they heard a roar from upstream, and someone cried out in alarm. When he looked up, he saw the river swelling. A crest of muddy water about two feet high was raging toward them. Terrified, he started to hurry toward the shore. Poor Little Fa of West Street cried out for all he was worth.

"Take me with you, Second Lock!" he screamed. "I can't run!"

But Second Lock couldn't run either; so he wasn't able to help Little Fa. Luckily, Uncle Fushan was on the threshing floor nearby. He rushed over with a wooden pitchfork in his hand and pulled Little Fa ashore with it. The boy was white with terror. . . .

But gradually Second Lock calmed down. The sea was quiet, with scarcely a ripple on it. The gulls were still circling low. When he looked at the sand castles, they hadn't budged. The water had neither risen nor fallen. Second

Lock had no idea how long he had been there and was beginning to grow sleepy. He dared not sleep, though, and started scooping up the sand by his side to keep himself awake. He dug down and down till he reached something hard and slippery. He sat up quickly to look. A big, colored clam!

He opened his mouth instinctively to call Tiger, but then he thought better of it. He'd collect a whole pile of clams to surprise Tiger when he came back. "Ha!" he said to himself. "He's not the only one who can find them."

Standing with legs wide apart, he bent down to dig again. In a little while he turned up another clam. He went on scooping, quite unaware of everything else. Sweat began to stream down his forehead, he broke his nails, and his fingers started to bleed; but he felt no pain at all. He tried to fix each clam in his memory so that he could tell his mother and sister when he got home which one was his first find, and which his second. . . .

The clams lay submissively on the sand, making no attempt to escape or even to stir. Still, Second Lock could not put his mind at ease. He moved them farther from the water, built a high rampart of sand around them, and covered it with his shirt and trousers.

He went on digging in a frenzy, placing more and more "prisoners" inside his rampart. At first he dug only nearby, to keep an eye on them. Then, confident that they could not escape, he started digging farther and farther away, only going back for a look when he had to escort new "prisoners." Later, he discovered he was wasting a lot of time carrying the clams there one by one. So he took his shirt with him and wrapped each new find in it, not going back each time till he had collected about ten.

Time plays curious tricks on us. Sometimes an hour seems longer than a day, and sometimes a day seems to pass in a matter of minutes. Second Lock was so absorbed in his work

39

that he quite lost track of the time; then he happened to raise his head and saw that the sun had moved quite far to the west. With a start he remembered the two sand castles. He raced back to have a look at them; but when he reached the shore he stood aghast. Not a trace of the castles could be seen: the stream had widened—the water in it was muddy.

Second Lock was horror-stricken. He rushed madly to and fro, waving his shirt and trousers and calling Tiger at the top of his lungs, though he could see no sign of him. A long time passed before Tiger appeared to his left. Second Lock shouted louder than ever and ran toward his cousin, often looking back over his shoulder at the estuary. How quickly the sea had changed! Water was surging up the beach, swallowing five feet or more in the flash of an eye. Now Tiger was running to meet him too, but how slow he seemed! Even a three-year-old could run faster than that.

When Tiger reached Second Lock, he understood everything at one glance and glared angrily at his cousin in silence. By this time, the tide had reached them. The stream of water was twice as wide as before. Second Lock looked at Tiger and burst into tears.

After a moment, Tiger said: "Never mind. Let's try it. Hold on to my foot, and I'll try to tow you across."

Second Lock stopped crying and followed him into the water. As soon as it reached their shoulders, Tiger began to swim; but when Second Lock seized one of his feet they both began to sink. Then Tiger grasped Second Lock's arm and helped him back to the shore. Too stunned now even to cry, Second Lock clutched at his cousin, who had also turned pale.

The foaming water was rising fast. It had nearly reached Second Lock's "prisoners" rampart. Catching sight of his cousin's white cotton trousers, Tiger snatched them up and tied the ends of the legs with his belt, then soaked them in the water, whirled them through the air and plunged them again in the tide. The legs, filled with air, floated up like water wings. Grasping the top of the trousers firmly, Tiger pulled Second Lock to him. Without a word he pushed him into the water and tucked the inflated legs beneath his arms.

"Hold on tight," he ordered. "Don't let go, whatever happens."

Using one arm to swim, with the other Tiger tugged Second

41

Lock after him, while the air in the improvised buoy hissed as it slowly leaked out.

What a difficult trip! Tiger swam painfully forward, foot by foot. By the time they were halfway across, the water wings were shrinking fast and Second Lock was slowly going under. But making one last great effort, Tiger swam three or four yards more and felt for the bottom. The water was only waist high! Second Lock nearly burst with joy as he waded ashore.

"Wait a second," said Tiger, "while I go back for our things."

He plunged once more into the water. Presently he returned with is own clothes and Second Lock's shirt, which held both boys' clams.

Second Lock kept up well as they raced toward the village. He had forgotten the pain in his feet and his exhaustion. On and on they ran. Soon they passed the rocks now half sub-

merged, and looking over his shoulder, Second Lock saw a
huge white sheet of rolling water. The sea was catching up
with them! Tiger told him that the current ran faster here
than south of their home, some two to three miles an hour.
Even so, they managed to outrun it, to Second Lock's im-
mense relief.

At last they were back in the village. A girl carrying two
buckets to the well laughed at them. "Aren't you ashamed
to run about naked?" she asked. "You'd better hurry home.
Tiger's father has been looking for you everywhere."

At the next tree, Tiger helped Second Lock untie his trousers, wring them out, and hang them on a branch to dry.

43

After scrambling into his own clothes he sat down gloomily on the grass, wondering how he could explain things to his father. Second Lock too was far from happy. To the north, a wide expanse of water met his eyes. Shuddering involuntarily, he looked at Tiger. What a wonderful fellow he was!

"Hey! You know something, Tiger?" he blurted out. "I like you ever so much. I really do. Let's be friends all our lives. What do you say?"

Tiger sat there without answering, gazing vaguely out to sea, frowning as he clasped his knees. After quite a long time he said: "If my father asks you any questions when we get back, don't tell him everything, understand? Just say I was the one who took you to the far shore of the estuary, that it wasn't your idea. . . ."

Tiger stood up and took hold of Second Lock's hand, and together the two boys ran on toward home.

Translated by Wen Feng
Illustrated by Zhou Si-cong

INDIA

The Red and Gold Shoe

by Margaret R. Bhatty

"Cock-a-doodle-doo! Cock-a-doodle-doo!" You'd think there ought to be a pleasanter way to wake up than by having the red cock Lalu split his sides crowing from under his reed basket in the middle of the floor of Amma's hut. And immediately the two foolish hens under their crate in a corner begin to fidget and cluck and knock on the wooden slats to be let out.

"Cock-a-doodle-doo!" and "Cluck! cluck! cluck!" This is the way a day begins for eight-year-old Lata where she sleeps on a tin trunk. Old Amma gropes from her string cot for the bamboo pole she keeps handy, and she waves it about as if she would drive back the dawn, for, oh! she is tired and aged and would so like to sleep a little longer.

" Whack! whack! whack!" She wallops the basket under which the cock crows. That ought to keep the red devil quiet. May a plague take him! May it wither his flesh and drain his bones dry! May it lock his joints and choke him—he and his cock-a-doodle-doo! He would bring the roof down on a tired old woman's head, would he? "Whack!"

But the signal has been given. Out from under Amma's cot comes Rakhi the goat and tweaks Lata's braids where she lies. In at the window drops Maow the wicked tomcat after another night of brawling with other cats in the fish market across the railway line, and outside the door whines Kalu the black dog who belongs to everyone in general but loves Lata and her grandmother in particular.

45

"Lata! Lata! Get up!" shrills Amma. "Let Lalu out! Let Kalu in! Go fetch the water!"

This is the way each day begins for Lata: Let-Lalu-out-let-Kalu-in, go-fetch-the-water! This is how the day always begins down by the railway yard, on your right as you ride grandly into the city gazing down from the height of the fine cream and blue carriages of the train called the Rani. The little lane is very crooked as only lanes can be, and the homes of the poor stand shoulder to shoulder along the slatted fencing of the railway. The houses may sag in places, but they have bravely held each other upright for many a year now.

"Is it time, Granny?" sleepy voices call from all sides. "But the Rani hasn't gone through yet, has it? Is it late then? Or has the moon turned your Lalu's brain? And Pinto Carpenter's alarm clock—has that rung yet?"

"Cock-a-doodle-doo!" replies the red cock, but his voice is drowned in the sudden thunder of the train. It rocks the tiny shacks, clatters the tin roofs, and shakes the rows of god pictures in their gaudy frames in each home—many-armed gods and goddesses, the elephant-headed, the monkey-headed, and the Virgin Mary, Queen of Heaven.

As if startled awake by the train, Pinto's alarm clock jumps with fright and begins to ring. It would turn red in the face if it could; but instead it hops angrily up and down on the shelf where it is tied to a nail with a piece of string. When the train has passed, it is still ringing. Everyone hears it and everyone knows that another day has indeed begun.

Lata was first at the water tap. She usually was because old Amma, her grandmother, went early to work in the homes of the rich beyond the station where she swept, scrubbed, and swabbed. She would return at noon with leftovers of food for Lata, the cock, hens, cat, goat, and dog, and then go off again to do the evening chores.

46

Lata never lingered at the tap. And certainly not today—
not when all the girls were talking about today's doll-marriage party. What will you wear? What are we getting to eat?
Never before had a match been arranged more grandly. The
plastic doll from the sweetseller's house was to be married to
the rubber doll from the betel seller's. Anyone would be
proud to get her doll married into the sweetseller's house, for
it was the richest in the lane, and the feast would be something to talk about for days afterwards. There would doubt-

less be pieces of stale milk fudge from the sweetseller's own shop, fried crisps, sesame crunch, and maybe even buttermilk only a day old. Lata was never invited to any weddings. She was shabby, she had no father, her mother was dead, and her grandmother worked as a domestic servant. She couldn't provide a feast for the neighborhood children because she lived on scraps off the tables of the rich.

When one is not invited to the most important function in one's street, just two doors away, there's no point standing around at the tap discussing it. So Lata hurried away as soon as her pot was full. She was never invited to any doll-marriage feast; but neither was she the only one. Six-year-old Joseph Pinto never attended because he couldn't walk after polio had left his legs useless. He sat on his bed in his house most of the time except when Lata came, as she did today, and carried him out on her back, creeping through a hole in the railway fence to the green grass on the other side. Here she gently set him down while Rakhi the goat went off to graze.

Jumping off the embankment, Rakhi trotted along the tracks, her hoofs tapping on the crossties as she went. "Rakhi! Come back!" Lata yelled. "And isn't the grass good enough right here?" It never was, for a goat always sees finer patches farther ahead, and off she goes. Rakhi was a city goat and knew how to look after herself.

The children's favorite place for playing was a hollow in the embankment where seasons ago mud had been dug out by men working on the line. The hollow was overgrown with short grass now, and Lata settled Joseph into it, drawing his legs out before him so that he could balance where he sat.

Leaning back, Joseph looked high into the sky where flights of snowy white egrets winged their way toward the lakes set in the rolling hills of a national park. Or he watched giant jet planes zoom over.

"When I grow up, I shall fly," he always said, repeating it

every day to make sure it would happen. Joseph planned to do everything that needed no legs. So he would fly like a jet plane, or an egret. Or he would drive a train. Engine drivers don't need legs, not with all those many wheels whirling so fast to carry them along.

Whenever a long-distance train thundered down the track, they watched it go, their hearts beating fast with excitement and a little fear. It made the ground heave and shake, and unable to contain themselves, Lata and Joseph yelled and shouted, waving madly at the startled faces of the passengers in the windows. As the train flew past, the invisible rush of its wings blew against their faces and lifted their hair. It was a thrilling moment but it never lasted long enough.

"When I grow up I shall be an engine driver," vowed

Joseph breathlessly, not looking at his legs lying side by side like the limp broken wings of a bird.

"Of course you will!" cried Lata, still feeling her heart thudding. "And will you wave to me as you go past?"

"I'll blow the whistle all the way through here and make Momin Sheikh's pigeons on the factory roof go straight up into the air with fright, and scatter the people in all directions, and shake old Amma's house so that she will shout: 'It's that devil Joseph again! Nobody else takes a train through here like that! He would bring the roof down on a tired old woman's head, would he?' "

Joseph was not really a boaster. He needed to talk big sometimes because he felt so small and unimportant the rest of the time.

Lata laughed as she hopped first on one foot and then on the other. It wasn't only because of the train that she was feeling like this. There was something else: she had a secret, and now that she had enjoyed it for long enough, she was going to tell it to Joseph.

Standing before him on the slope, she said: "I have ten coppers!"

"From where?" he cried in pleased surprise as she held up the coin.

"Amma gave it to me before she left for work."

Here was wealth indeed! One whole ten-copper coin! And now came the sweet agony of trying to decide how to spend it in such a way that they wouldn't be sorry afterwards. It was terrible to have to say: "Those peanuts were not so good, were they? We should have bought the cotton candy—one ball for you and one for me." But then how to be absolutely sure? Cotton candy went much too fast, and it left only a little taste of sweetness behind. Puffed rice went further. And a twist of toffee pulled off the vendor's pole and shaped into a butterfly or a bird stuck to the teeth and went even further.

50

While a lemon drop could last for days if you sucked it only now and then and kept it wrapped in a piece of paper in your pocket.

"What will you buy?" asked Joseph seriously, for he knew this problem called for much thought.

Lata was quite sure what she would do. "We'll have a doll marriage too, and we'll have a feast." So what if they'd not been invited? A marriage and a feast of their own would make things equal. Well, almost equal—for it couldn't be much of a marriage when one had no dolls. The groom was the wooden handle of a chisel with the blade snapped off from Joseph's house, and the bride was the short stout stick with which Lata's grandmother beat the clothes at the pond. Both stood stiffly side by side against the fence, with eyes, a nose, and a mouth put on with a charred stick. For ten coppers the feast had to be modest indeed, with roasted peas served in silver cups made from paper out of empty cigarette boxes they found along the tracks.

They ate the peas slowly and very solemnly. It would not do to gobble them too fast, for once they were gone the feast would be over. Too soon would their pleasure become a thing of the past. The peas had to be chewed and tasted to the fullest so that they could be remembered to the fullest.

"We won't tell anybody—not anybody," said Lata, munching.

"No, we won't tell anybody," Joseph repeated, nodding his head, for there is always a certain pride in the possession of a secret of one's very own. However, the real truth was that it hadn't been much of a marriage. The others would laugh out loud, and that they could not have borne.

What with all the preparation—hunting for tinfoil, running to the station to buy the peas from the old man at the grade crossing there, and setting up the bride and bride-groom, the children were unaware of how the time had

51

passed until Lata heard her grandmother calling from the lane on the other side of the fence.

But where was the goat? "Rakhi! Rakhi!" she cried, jumping to her feet.

"She was down that way." Joseph said, pointing along the tracks as Lata set off.

If luck were something one could be sure of, there wouldn't be any fun to it. "If Rakhi hadn't strayed so far that day, we would never have found the shoe," Lata always said later, convinced it was all because of their good luck.

She was running along the tracks, not even looking down, when the gleam caught her eye. All crimson and gold, it flashed in the afternoon sun. And when she went over and picked it up, her eyes opened wide in astonishment and delight. A child's shoe—and what a shoe! Of soft red velvet it was, with a leather sole and worked all over from end to end with gold thread. The toe tapered to a fine golden point and then curved back on itself. What was more, it was brand-new. Perhaps its mate lies somewhere close by, thought Lata, as she searched along the tracks and among the bushes. But she didn't find it. There was only one shoe. Nevertheless, when you have never owned a pair of shoes in your life, even one is better than none.

There was nothing magical about the shoe. What magic can there be in a thing thrown out of the window of a passing train by a willful spoiled child who should have known better? But then again, what is magic if it isn't marvel and change and all the difference between the ordinary and the extraordinary?

The change began working from that very day. Now there is a way of wearing only one shoe so that nobody will suspect it is only half of a pair. Or better still, there is a way to make it appear that wearing only one is the most natural thing in the world, and the only reason why more people don't do it is because other shoes are made for walking. This shoe was not.

Every evening Lata carried little Joseph Pinto out to a stone bench in the nearby park where he could watch the others play. It isn't a park really—only a half-hearted attempt at a park in the open space behind the shantytown where the city ends and the countryside begins. The statue in the center is of the man who first had the idea and gave the piece of land. But he died soon after and the rest of the money was spent on this statue, while the park was left unfinished. He is a tall stout figure of a man standing on a platform, and Momin Sheikh's pigeons, the sparrows, crows, and other birds have made a sorry mess of him. He is surrounded by a dozen or more small concrete posts from which it was planned to sling heavy chains, but the money was used up and everyone lost interest in the scheme. Janak Seth, he is called, and the children have made up a song that they sing as they play a game of their own around him:

Janak Rajah went to Dilli,
Brought back thirteen bowls of gold,
Thirteen bowls for thirteen children,
Some still hungry, some still cold.

The one who is chosen to be the rajah climbs onto the platform and takes his place between the broad feet of Janak Seth, holding a long stick in his hand. The others skip around and sing the jingle. When the rajah brings his stick down to strike the closest post, there is a scramble to get to any one of the posts surrounding the statue. There is much laughter and yelling, much shoving, pushing, and hair pulling along with wrenching at each other's clothes. Arguments often grow so bitter that some don't speak to each other for days afterward because all those who don't get to a pillar and cling to it for dear life are declared "out" by the rajah. However, in the next general scramble they usually get right back into the game. And so it goes, endlessly.

Lata had never been chosen rajah and so she naturally thought it was a silly game. "It's the stupidest game I ever saw and I refuse to play it," she said since she wasn't given any place in the playing of it. "Yes," echoed little Joseph, to whom all such games had to seem silly, "it's the stupidest game I ever saw." So the two of them always pretended to be more interested in watching the big boys playing marbles or tipcat.

That evening Lata sat with one leg neatly folded under her, while the other hung down wearing the red and gold shoe. She swung her leg back and forth so that from the corner of an eye she could see it flash out. And sometimes she held her leg stiffly out before her as if she'd forgotten to

54

swing it back. As she had hoped, she soon had a small knot of children gaping at her where she sat, though she pretended not to notice them.

"Where did you get such a grand pair of shoes?" asked one of the children in astonishment.

Lata didn't answer or even turn her head from watching the game of tipcat; but she was aware that more children were running across to join the crowd, until the sweetseller's daughter, who was then the rajah, was left perched alone on Janak Seth's feet and feeling very annoyed about it. Finally, she climbed down and pushed her way through the others to stand before Lata and Joseph.

Where did you get them? Is it real gold—all that thread? Who gave them to you? For a while Lata enjoyed the sensation and then she and Joseph looked at each other and smiled all over their faces, the way we do when we're very pleased about something and don't care who knows it.

"My grandmother bought them for me," Lata said serenely, pulling her shabby skirt straight to make sure that the other foot was well hidden from view.

"My father could buy a dozen such shoes," sniffed the sweetseller's girl.

"Perhaps," responded Lata, "but he hasn't done so yet, has he?"

She held out her foot, turning the ankle a bit to let them all get a good look. The shoe wasn't a good fit. In fact it hurt a bit—but for the sensation it was causing it was well worth a pinched toe or two.

"It's beautiful pair of shoes," someone breathed.

"But there's only one!" burst out the simple-hearted Joseph before Lata could stop him.

Only one? How silly! Only one shoe! Shoes always come in pairs, don't they?

"Yes, but this isn't for walking in. It's a shoe for show,"

chattered Joseph, for all this sudden success had quite gone to his little head.

"Hear that!" sneered the sweetseller's daughter. "Only one shoe and that only for show! You should know all about that, O Legless One!"

Poor Joseph's face fell, for he always felt sensitive about his sorry legs.

"It is too!" cried Lata stoutly. "It's not for walking. See?"

Slipping it off she turned it over to show them the underside still smooth and unsoiled. And inside there was a soft sole of gray felt. "It's a shoe only for show."

It certainly was, and she was not going to waste her time arguing with anyone who refused to believe the evidence of his eyes "Have you ever seen anyone *walking* in such shoes?" Along the dusty lanes of their shantytown? Through the slush by the water tap, and the coal dust, and the litter, and the cattle droppings? Of course they hadn't!

They passed the shoe from hand to hand, and Lata watched jealously as they examined it.

"Can I try it on?" asked one of the girls, and Lata looked at her for a long moment. "Only for a second—just to see what it feels like," the girl pleaded.

This was something new indeed—to be asked, instead of ordered, shouted at, or even pushed. And then to know that she had the choice of answering yes, or even no. She had to be careful here, and so she said, with that cunning that comes from being treated like nothing for too long: "What will you give me in return?"

It started off with a piece of sesame crunch saved from the recent marriage feast to which they had not invited her. She shared it promptly with Joseph, and from there it went on until, at the end of the week, she had for him a top without a point, three plastic bangles for herself, first place at the tap on two occasions when she overslept and was late, and even an invitation to a not-so-important doll marriage.

For only the first week that was a good run of luck indeed, and Lata had reason to feel happy. The conditions laid down for the wearing of her shoe were stern. It must never touch the ground, nor be scuffed against anything to wear away the gold. This was no ordinary shoe and therefore it must be treated as no ordinary shoe was ever treated. Such conditions were bound to affect the wearer too. The betel seller's daughter borrowed the shoe for a whole afternoon and she wore it when her relatives called on the family from their village. All through the visit she sat sedately on a trunk, one leg folded under her and the other hanging down.

"What a beautiful pair of shoes!" cried her girl cousins, green with envy.

"What a modest and well-behaved girl!" said the elders —which she certainly was not. But for this excellent piece of foolery, the shoe earned Lata twenty-five coppers, with which she and Joseph treated themselves to gaudy pink balls of ice on sticks. They never bought these things because, as they argued—after they were eaten—it was nothing but frozen water after all, wasn't it? And they had to be eaten fast; otherwise they melted down one's chin and were wasted. However, now Lata and Joseph could allow themselves such extravagance because the shoe held out promise of more to come.

"If we sold it, we could easily get a thousand rupees!" cried Joseph, his eyes shining.

Perhaps that was wishful thinking—but being rajah no longer was, and it was a proud moment when Lata was allowed to climb to the coveted position between Janak Seth's broad feet, wearing the shoe and holding the stick aloft to start the game. Shabby she was, and shabby she would remain—but at last she had something about which

58

she could feel important. And this the shoe had done for her.

Unfortunately even the most enchanted of shoes have a way of growing too small for one's feet, and there came a time when Lata couldn't wear her gold and red shoe any more. The felt innersole had become dirty from all the grubby feet that had worn it, the gold thread was not so gold any more, and the whole shoe had begun to show wear and even a little tear in its velvet. But even if Lata and every other child in the lane outgrew it, there was still one person not likely to do so. With a little wad of paper stuffed into its toe, the shoe would always fit Joseph. That was the way he wore it the first time Lata lifted him into place between Janak Seth's broad feet. Sitting under the gentle curve of Seth's large round stomach, he seemed smaller than ever, but he was smiling.

He looked down and all the faces were turned up to him. To think that he, poor little Joseph Pinto the Legless One had the power in this hand that held the rod to make all those children stop or go just as he chose! The thought almost brought tears to his eyes.

"Joseph is rajah!" cried Lata, clapping her hands. "Joseph is rajah forever!"

"Janak Rajah went to Dilli . . ." the children chanted.

So Joseph too became a rajah, and because of his shriveled legs, it was possible he might be rajah forever. This was far better than pretending to believe he could ever become a jet-plane pilot, or an egret, or even an engine driver.

Illustrated by Yusuf Lien

The Rhinoceros Hunt

by Moh. Ambri

Editors' Note. This story was originally written in Sundanese, the language of western Java, in 1932. Most of the people there are Muslims and observe the fast of Ramadan, the month during which no one eats or smokes between sunrise and sunset each day. The rhinoceroses of this story are a rare species with a single horn, found only in Java. The breed is now in danger of extinction and is being protected by the government.

That morning I woke up late. It was just after eight, and the day was already getting hot. I was very hungry, but even after I'd had a bath there was still no sign of anyone with my breakfast. Curious, I went out into the garden and walked around the house to look in the kitchen windows. There wasn't even the smell of cooking. Wondering what was the matter, I lit a cigarette.

Just then Momo and Datje came into the garden. Seeing me, they stopped and Momo said, as though surprised: "Why are you smoking?"

"Oh," I said, "I always have a cigarette just before breakfast."

"But this is the first day of Ramadan," he said.

With a start I realized he was right. "How could I have forgotten?" I said.

"Oh, well," said Momo, "if you forgot, it's all right."

"But I really don't feel like fasting. I'm very hungry, and besides, I forgot to say my Ramadan prayers last night."

Datje cut in: "If you don't feel like fasting, just say so. No use making a fuss about it."

"Well, as a matter of fact, I've been longing for breakfast ever since I woke up."

"All right, then," said Datje, "let's go see if there aren't some leftovers from yesterday."

The three of us went into the deserted kitchen. After looking around, Datje found some stale rice and soup, but it didn't seem at all appetizing; so he went to look in the pantry. In a minute he came back and said: "All the cupboards are locked."

"Isn't there some eating stall nearby?" asked Momo.

"Now why would there be a stall open on the first day of Ramadan?" said Datje. "But we might try looking in the storage shed."

We left the kitchen and, as we were passing the plantation office, heard old Suanta talking. Other people were laughing.

We turned into the room, and Datje said: "What's so funny?"

Someone said: "Suanta is telling one of his adventures, about being chased by a rhino."

We said we would like to hear the story too and asked Suanta to start again.

"With pleasure," answered Suanta. "I was only telling the exciting part, but now I'll begin at the beginning."

And here is his tale:

This was many years ago when I was still young. There was a rumor that some rhinos were in a nearby forest. So our master—Datje's father—sent a man who knew the forest well to have a look, and also sent two or three hunters to search for the rhinos' footprints. The men came back and said there was no doubt about it: the prints the animals had left around Tjibeureum Swamp were much deeper than those

62

of a buffalo. So the master sent a report to the provincial and district authorities.

Within three days the viceroy and other high officials of the district came for a rhino hunt. Our master summoned the headmen of the surrounding villages, together with many hunters and trackers and porters, as an escort for the dignitaries.

After everyone had gathered together at dawn, we set out for the forest. The officials were on horseback and the village people followed behind, carrying spears and knives and bamboo drums. Porters carried food in bags and baskets made of bark and string; otherwise, they were unarmed except for their machetes.

Now, hunting rhinos is quite different from hunting other animals. You have to set up a base of operations in the forest and bring enough food for three or four days. So we brought along many bags of rice and pots to cook it in, besides the rice that was already prepared.

"And what was your load?" I asked.

"Nothing," the old man answered, "all I had to carry was the master's rifle and ammunition."

"So you didn't carry any food?"

"No, those of us who were personal attendants of the master had to depend upon him for our food. But he was always very generous about giving us plenty of leftovers."

And the old man went on with his story:

It was still morning when we reached the forest; the day was just beginning to get hot. We started building some huts, strong enough for overnight shelter, in a wide, open field. When the villagers arrived, they were divided into several groups. Then they set out in different directions, leaving behind only the men working on the huts. Each group was led by a village headman and an official with a rifle. There were about twenty rifles in all.

The viceroy and the rest of the officials set off for the place of ambush. This was an open field where a platform already stood—no, not just a platform, but more of a hut built above the ground with live trees for poles. Branches that had grown around the hut were cut away to give a good view, and the riflemen climbed into the hut to wait. It was a very pleasant place for an ambush. If a rhino showed himself anywhere in that vicinity, a single well-aimed shot would soon bring him down.

64

All day long the bamboo drums could be heard faintly in the distance as the beaters searched for the rhinos; it seemed as though the sound would never end. Nothing happened all that first day. Things began again the next morning; the surrounding circle of beaters with their drums grew gradually smaller. But again night came without any sign of a rhino.

Early in the morning of the third day people came from a nearby plantation and reported that some rhinos had come into their village the night before. Trackers were sent to have a look and they came back saying the animals had gone from the village into the forest near our ambush.

Beaters surrounded this part of the forest, and trackers kept on the move to make sure the animals had not slipped out of the forest. Everyone felt sure that the rhinos were inside the circle of beaters. The hunters who had picked the ambush spot were highly praised for having chosen so well. Everyone waited anxiously.

Fires were lit on the south and east sides of the forest. There was a strong wind and the fire blazed high, sending smoke up into the sky. To the west there was shouting, and the drums kept beating loudly. The fire spread quickly, its flames licking out in all directions, thundering and roaring and blackening the sky. When the fire from the east joined that from the south, the smoke billowed still higher. The circle of beaters kept growing smaller, and presently the sound of loud rifle fire was heard over the shouting and the drums.

It was terribly frightening: sitting on a branch with your heart thumping, trying to keep as still as possible. I got down and joined the shouting crowd.

We could hear the rhinos coming from the burning forest. A crowd of people came shouting toward the dry field, over-grown with weeds and small trees. There were only a few

tall trees. The rhinos suddenly appeared from the east, looking like huge, rolling boulders.

People were shouting: "Rhino! Rhino!" The drums grew louder.

The rhinos kept on walking to the west. There were three of them: a male, a female, and one offspring. When they saw people surrounding them, they turned back toward the east and stopped again when they reached the edge of the forest. They seemed to be afraid of the fire, and the smoke was suffocating; so they turned back to the west but were blocked by the people. In the end, looking bewildered, the rhinos stood in the middle of the dry field. There was no doubt that the biggest one was a male. It bellowed, its mouth wide open. God! I can still remember the terrible redness of its mouth and its dreadful teeth.

The dignitaries shouted orders, telling the people to move closer. Flames and smoke billowed in a tall black wall. The weeds were burnt to a crisp. The rhinos were already troubled, sensing that they were in danger. The only way out was to the north. But strangely they did not want to run that way. It was as if they had sensed our presence. They seemed to be thinking, gazing toward the southwest horizon. It was then half past five. A bamboo trumpet sounded. Like a startled daydreamer, the male rhino roared, then dashed to the west. Ignoring the shouts of the people, it ran on, plunging into the crowd. Then the rhino bellowed again, calling for its child and wife. The three ran in a line, the child in the middle, and they escaped through a gap in the crowd.

The people were stunned. Many of them fell in their haste to run away. I lost my head too. I ran and climbed one of the tall trees, then hung on tightly and closed my eyes. The rhinos seemed to be right below me, heaving deep breaths. I felt dizzy, lost my grip on the tree and fell on the rhino's back, it seemed.

I had fallen on Lahiam, who had been crawling around at the foot of the tree. It had been Lahiam panting a while ago, not the rhino. Lahiam winced and complained that his back hurt.

The others had been just as frightened as I had. Lahiam had been unable to stand up. I heard there were even some who couldn't help peeing in their pants.

It was the hunters who ran the fastest and were the first

to climb trees. There was a dignitary from the town who was said to be brave. But when he saw the rhinos approaching, he quickly flung his rifle away and climbed the nearest tall tree.

"The rifle, sir, the rifle!!" people yelled to him. And what was his reply? "You can take the rifle and use your eyes for bullets!"

The rhinos had vanished; we could no longer even hear them. Everyone climbed down from the trees and gathered together. With the rhinos a safe distance away, their courage reappeared and they told each other tall tales. Then we returned to the base camp. The viceroy felt very guilty, having blown the trumpet to stop the people from getting too close to the rhinos but having startled the rhinos instead. Thinking it impossible to pursue them, he dismissed the party right then. At about 9:00 P.M. we set off for home. We arrived here just when the drum for the dawn meal was being beaten.

Bad luck! Having taken all that trouble, we returned from the hunt empty-handed. All the way home, whenever I saw something black crouching by the side of the road, my heart jumped. It always seemed to be the rhinos.

"Maybe your luck is as bad as mine, Suanta," I said. "How big was the male rhino?"

Suanta replied: "Oh, it was big, sir, bigger than a buffalo. It was about ten feet long, with a thick neck, a bald head, and a large snout. It had a crooked horn, sir, very frightening, but you couldn't see its eyes."

"And what were its teeth like?" asked Momo.

"I don't know. I couldn't see clearly, but if I haven't forgotten, its teeth were like a pig's, only much bigger. Oh, it was really terrible!"

"And how big was the baby rhino?" I asked.

69

"Oh, small, sir, about the size of a young buffalo. I've really had enough of rhinos! If the master ever wants to take me on a hunt again, I won't join in as quickly as I did last time."

Translrted by Ati K. Hadimadja
Illustrated by Syahwil

IRAN

The Story of Helly

by Nader Ebrahimi

It wasn't a thousand years ago, nor a hundred years either. It was just two years ago or maybe last year. In our neighborhood, in our lane, there lived a girl whose name was Helly, and she was eight years old. As a matter of fact, in our neighborhood, in our lane, many boys and girls were living.

There was a girl named Zari. Zari did embroidery and a little housework. She also washed dishes, brought tea, and washed the cups and saucers occasionally, but she could not clean greasy plates very well.

Another girl was called Lilly. She sang songs. She had memorized several long songs. Whenever anyone asked her, she would sing one of these songs. But she never sang when she was by herself, nor did she sing when her brother was studying or doing his homework.

Another girl was called Mehri. She liked to play with flowers and arrange them in vases. Often she would get herself wet by spilling water from the vases, but she never got other people wet.

And there was the boy Taghi. He used to build tiny houses out of boards and nails and paint them with watercolors. He never bothered anyone. And he never played with his houses until he had finished his homework.

And there were many, many others. There was Mahvash and Mahshid, Khosrow and Jamshi, Maryam and Mitra, Houshang and Reza, Manijeh and. . . . They all lived in our neighborhood and were always busy doing something.

71

Now let me tell you about Helly. Everyone in the neighborhood called her Naughty Helly. It seemed as though there was nothing in the world she could do except bother people —bother her mother and father, bother her sister and brother, bother, bother. No sooner would she get home from school than her mother would be yelling: "Helly, don't touch the dishes. Helly, don't put on my shoes. Helly, don't tease Hormoz. Helly, don't make faces. Helly, don't come in the room wearing Goli's shoes. Helly, don't play with the kerosene lamp. Helly, don't act so spoiled. . . ."

But Helly never listened to her mother or anyone else. She was always doing things at the wrong time. When it was time for sleeping she would start singing. When it was time for lunch she would go out into the lane. She always made noise in the classroom, and in winter she was always throwing snowballs at people.

Sometimes she ran out into the lane and bothered the grocer—or the carpenter—or the street sweeper. The sweeper was such a kind, good-hearted man that Helly bothered him a lot. The man who sold lottery tickets in the lane was always angry with Helly. Even the kind dog Hoffy, who lived in our lane, had to stay awake all the long hot summer afternoons on the lookout for Helly, who was sure to hurt him if she found him asleep.

So, as I was going to say, there was nobody in our neighborhood, in our lane, who liked Helly. Not the ticket seller, not the street sweeper, nor the butcher, nor the carpenter, nor the other children—nobody liked her, and they all complained about her to her mother.

One evening a wise old man from a distant city came to visit Helly's mother. She told the old man how Helly bothered everyone, even the dog, and how nobody liked her.

The old man thought for a while and then said: "You know, I think your daughter doesn't appreciate her home and

her neighborhood. If she did, she wouldn't be always bothering everyone. The trouble is that she has never been sad and unhappy because she was lonely. Now, I think you should send her somewhere far from home where she would be by herself and very, very lonely."

Helly's mother laughed and said: "How could I send her away? Where could I send her to be lonely? Is there a place where no one could hear her voice and her crying? Where? Where?"

The old man said: "Well, send her along to me and you'll see how well I manage things."

Helly's mother laughed and said: "But I love her so much. How could I bear parting with her?"

Helly was in the same room, busily tying up the legs of their white cat with some string. Now, hearing their conversation, she turned pale and let the cat go. She was suddenly afraid and went to one corner of the room where she was very, very silent.

Presently the old man went to bed. Then Helly ran to her mother, hugged her, and between sobs said: "Mother, Mother. I don't want to be lonely. Please don't send me away. Please don't send me to a place where nobody can even hear my voice."

Heartbroken by this plea, Helly's mother kissed her and caressed her smooth black hair and said, laughing: "Look, Helly, I promise not to send you anywhere if only you'll listen to what I say and don't throw water on people, and don't throw stones at the dog, and don't mark up the walls, and don't yell all the time, and don't cry, and don't make noise at school, and don't throw snowballs at people. And now you'd better go to bed so you can get up early in the morning."

Helly went to bed, but she still kept worrying about what the old man had said. She thought: "What if Mother really

75

does send me away to some far place? What if she sends me to this old man? What if the old man turns me into a bird or a cockroach or an ant or a tree in a flowerbed? . . ."

While she was thinking and thinking, Helly fell asleep. No sooner had her eyes closed than she began dreaming.

She was walking with her mother along a broad path in a big, green, and flowery garden. She asked her mother: "What place is this?"

Her mother answered: "This is the old man's garden."

But Helly couldn't believe that her mother would leave her here all alone in a green and flowery garden. So she laughed and said: "I'm the way I am and as long as I live I won't change. If you leave me here, I'll bother the old man so much that he'll get sick and tired of me and send me back home."

Helly's mother said nothing and took her to the old man. He lived in a white marble palace in the center of the garden. Her mother greeted the old man, sat down, and said: "Well, old man, I'll leave my girl here with you. When she's learned to behave herself you can send her home." Then she got up, said good-bye, and started to leave.

Helly yelled: "Mother, Mother! I don't want to stay with this old man. I don't want to stay here."

But her mother made no reply. She walked on into the garden and disappeared among the flowers and trees.

The old man said to Helly: "Well, baby, come here. So here you are and here you stay. Now where would you like to live?"

Helly, feeling very sad and lonely, answered: "It makes no difference to me. I'm the way I am and as long as I live I won't change."

The old man laughed and said: "I tell you, there're ways to make you change your mind. I'll turn you into a chicken

76

and send you to live in a cage with the other birds—with the hens and the roosters and the doves. Let's see if you can bother them."

Helly said: "I'm the way I am and as long as I live I won't change. I'll peck the chickens and the doves, peck their eyes right out."

The old man only looked at her. Then he raised his head and called out: "Can you hear me, hens? Can you hear me, roosters? Can you hear me, doves? Here's Helly, whom I'm leaving with you. Let us see how she gets along with all of you."

Helly sat herself down on the ground, saying: "I'm the way I am and as long as I live I won't change." But as she spoke she was turning into a short-legged chicken. Instead of her smooth black hair, she now had a black crest on her head. Instead of her bright red dress, her body was now covered with red feathers.

The old man called a boy and said to him: "Take this short-legged, black-crested, red-feathered hen and lock her up in the bird cage."

The boy caught Helly by the legs and threw her into the cage, which was made of gold and silver.

The chickens and the doves in the cage took one look at Helly and didn't like her at all. They flew at her and pecked at her head and clawed at her back. It was terrible, and soon she had a bad headache. She cried and wept, she sat down and she stood up, and she could see that the roosters were much stronger than she. Then she ran away into a distant corner of the cage and tried to take refuge from the other birds.

Presently the boy brought some grain to feed the birds. They swarmed around the feeding tray and began gobbling up the grain. When Helly came and tried to get a bite, they flew at her again. And again she had to retreat to the far corner of the cage, where she sat and thought how hungry she was.

She said to herself: "What a world! What a horrible world! Nobody ever worries about me. Nobody ever thinks that I too need food and water. I'm all alone here."

Then she went and asked the other birds to please give her some of the grain and let her have some water, but they didn't answer. None of the hens and roosters and doves took pity on her. Instead, whenever Helly came near them they would peck her on the head. They pecked her so much that part of the crest fell off her head. And finally she quit talking entirely, she quit walking around, she quit pecking, and she quit begging for food and water. All she did was sit in her far corner of the cage and murmur: "What a world! What a horrible world! No water, no food."

One day she remembered the old man and said to herself: "I wish he were here now and would ask how I'm feeling. I'd tell him, all right, how horrible everything is. I'd tell him I'd do anything he wanted, go wherever he wanted me to go, if only he would set me free and let me be happy again."

At this moment the old man appeared before her. Stretching out his hand, he pulled Helly out of the cage and asked: "How are you feeling, Helly?"

"Horrible!" answer Helly, "just horrible!"

The old man said: "Didn't I tell you couldn't cope with the birds? Just see how hard they've pecked at you until even a part of your crest fell off! Here, have a look at yourself in a mirror."

All of a sudden Helly changed back into her own shape. But her face was pale and she'd lost some of her black hair and she was very, very thin.

The old man held up a mirror and said: "Where's your smooth black hair? Where's your beautiful face? So now you know how uncomfortable it can be away from your own home."

Helly looked in the mirror and felt very sad. She said: "Old man, please save me from those birds. Please send me back home."

The old man answered: "No, it's still too soon. You still don't really appreciate your home. So choose some place else to live here. There are many nice places in this big garden. There're many flowers and there're parrots and nightingales. The parrots talk and the nightingales sing."

Helly answered: "I don't want a garden full of flowers. I don't want parrots and nightingales. I simply want to go home."

The old man said: "No, I'll send you any place you want to go in my garden, but you can't go home until you appreciate it."

"Well then," said Helly, "at least put me where there are other children to play with."

The old man said: "All right, if that's what you want. But what will happen if you start bothering them?"

"Oh," said Helly, "I promise not to do that." But to herself she said: "Maybe I couldn't cope with the birds but I can certainly handle children. I'll make them so tired of me they'll beg the old man to send me home."

But the old man knew what she was thinking and said: "So it's to the children you go, but you won't be able to talk to them. They'll be able to look at you but not to hear anything you say." Then he closed his eyes and said: "Let this little girl be turned into a picture, a picture of a little girl just like Helly, a picture in a book for children."

"No, no," Helly shouted. But even as she was speaking she became smaller and smaller, and then she suddenly found that she had become a picture in a picture book. The name of the book was *The Story of Helly*.

79

Then the old man took the book to a bookshop and asked the owner of the shop to sell it.

The Story of Helly, with the picture of Helly in it, was in the bookshop for a long, long time. It became all dusty, and no matter how she shouted, she was only a picture and no one could hear her voice.

Finally one day a young boy picked up the book and decided to buy it. He took the book home and showed it to the children in his neighborhood. Helly tried and tried to call out to them, but they couldn't hear a word she said.

One day when the boy was reading the book he stopped to look at the picture of Helly. He said: "But she's so pale. I know what I'll do—I'll color her." So he got out his colored pencils and started coloring Helly. The pencils were very sharp and hurt Helly's face very much. Shouting out with pain, she began wishing very hard that the old man would come. She'd tell him how sorry she was and promise to be good.

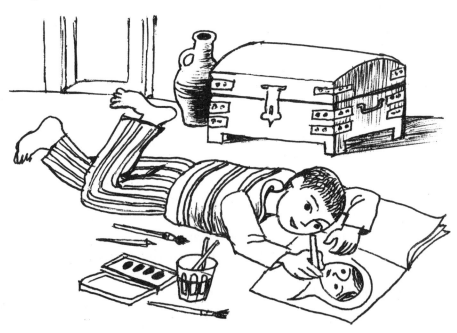

At this moment the old man appeared and said loudly: "Helly, come here to me. I want to talk to you. Come out of that book."

And suddenly Helly was out of the book and back in the garden. The old man asked her how she was and if she had had a good time with the other children.

Looking around at the garden, the birds, and the sky, Helly said: "How can I tell you, old man? My whole body hurts horribly. I've been colored yellow, blue, green, red, white, black, purple, and pink. Please take pity on me. Isn't it time for me to go home now?"

The old man said: "No, Helly. It's still too soon for you to go home. You don't really appreciate it yet. So where would you like to live now? There are many nice places in my garden here. The garden is full of parrots and nightingales. And there's my beautiful palace. What else could you want?"

Helly answered: "Please, old man, let me go, and keep your garden for yourself. Keep your old flowers and parrots and nightingales. I don't want to live in a white marble palace. Please send me back to my own home. Please, please!"

But the old man shook his head and said: "No, not home, but I'll send you any place else that you want."

Helly said: "Well, then, send me back to play with the other children, but please make it so that they can hear my voice."

The old man said: "All right, then, that's what I'll do."

Helly said to herself: "If the children can hear me, I'll scream so hard that they'll get tired of me and ask the old man to send me home."

But the old man knew what she was thinking and said: "All right, I'll make it so the children not only can hear you but will like your screams as well."

Then he said with a loud voice: "Helly, become a sounding-

81

iron." And with these words Helly found that she had been turned into a big flat piece of iron.

Then the old man took Helly to the nearby schoolyard and hung her up by a chain to be used as a school bell. When it was time for recess, the school janitor took a big club and banged on the sounding-iron so hard that Helly shouted: "My belly! My belly! Ding, dang, dong!" Over and over again: "My belly! My belly! Ding, dang, dong!"

And at the sound of Helly's screams the children ran out of their classrooms onto the playground. They clapped their hands, laughed, played, and danced, delighted to be outdoors and free of their studies.

Thus day after day Helly's voice rang out, screamed out. "My belly! My belly! Ding, dang, dong!" Helly could see the children playing, hear their laughter and shouting. And she would ring out again when it was time for them to go home, leaving her all alone. All the children could plainly hear her voice and were delighted with the sounds she made. And there she hung, day after day, and there wasn't a thing she could do about it.

One day after school was over and Helly had been left all alone, she fell to thinking: "What a hard life, being away from home! If only I could go home again, I'd be a perfect little girl." Remembering the old man, she thought: "Maybe he'll take pity on me and set me free. Maybe he'll ask where I want to live once more."

And suddenly she heard the old man's voice, saying: "Helly, come here. It seems you're beginning to see what wonderful places they were—your neighborhood and your lane and your home. Now you appreciate your home."

Looking around, Helly saw that she was back in her own shape, in the garden with the old man. She said hello and, very politely, asked after his health. Then she said: "Old man, please send me back home. Life is really too hard away

82

from home. If you'll let me go back, I promise to be a perfect little girl."

The old man said: "All right, I think you've learned your lesson. Since you don't seem to like my flowery garden, nor my parrots and nightingales, I'll let you go home. But your

head is covered with rust—where is your smooth black hair. And you're pale from so much screaming—where is your beautiful face? Just wait a minute and I'll restore your health; then I'll send you home."

The old man closed his eyes and said loudly: "Let Helly be young and beautiful just as she was the first day she came here."

Helly looked and saw that everything was as before, as though she had just stepped into the garden. And there, coming out of the distant flowers, was her mother running toward her. Helly ran to meet her. They hugged each other, crying with happiness and laughing with joy.

Helly said: "Mother, Mother, please don't send me away from home any more. I don't want a garden full of flowers. I don't want parrots and nightingales. I don't want to be painted, nor to be hit 'ding, dang, dong.' Please take me home. . . ."

Helly's mother was shaking Helly and saying: "Helly, Helly,

wake up. It's morning and the sun is shining. You've had quite enough sleep."

Helly looked around and asked: "Mother, where am I?"

Her mother answered: "You're in bed, at home. Where else do you think you would be?"

Helly sighed with relief. She laughed and jumped out of bed. She washed her face, dressed, ate breakfast, and ran to school. She didn't even remember the old man who was still asleep in the guest room, and she'd never have to see him again.

In the lane she bowed to the ticket seller and said: "Sir, please give me a ticket." The ticket seller laughed and said: "What makes you so polite today, Helly?"

Helly answered: "Because I'm a perfect little girl. That's the way I am and as long as I live I won't change."

Is it one or two years that have passed since Helly had her dream? She has gotten older, more helpful around the house, and kinder than ever before. Well, sometimes when she waters the flowers she spills water on herself, but she never splashes it on other people.

Oh, and by the way, I forgot to say that the dog Hoffy no longer limps: nobody throws stones at him any more and he can now sleep away the long hot summer afternoons.

Translated by Mehdi Ansari
Illustrated by Parviz Kalantari

The Kenju Wood

by Kenji Miyazawa

With his kimono fastened by a piece of rope and a smile on his face, Kenju would often stroll through the woods or along the paths between the fields. When he saw the green thickets in the rain, his eyes would twinkle with pleasure, and when he caught sight of a hawk soaring up and up into the blue sky he would jump for pure joy and clap his hands to tell everyone about it.

But the children made such fun of him that in time he began to pretend not to laugh. When a gust of wind came and the leaves on the beech trees shimmered in the light so that his face could not help smiling with pleasure, he would force his mouth open and take big, heavy breaths to hide his smiles as he stood gazing and gazing up into the boughs.

Sometimes as he laughed his silent laugh with his mouth wide open, he would rub his cheek with his finger, as though it itched. Seen from a distance, Kenju looked as though he was scratching his face or maybe yawning, but if you got close to him you could hear he was laughing and see that his lips were twitching. So the children made fun of him just the same.

If his mother had told him to, he could have drawn as many as five hundred buckets full of water at one time. He could have weeded the fields too in a single day. But his mother and father never told him to do such things.

Behind Kenju's house, there lay a stretch of open ground, as big as the average sports field, that had been left uncultivated. One year, while the mountains were still white with snow and the new grass had yet to put out buds on the plain, Kenju suddenly came running up to the other members of his family who were tilling the rice fields, and said: "Mother, please buy me seven hundred cedar seedlings."

Kenju's mother stopped wielding her gleaming new hoe and stared at Kenju. "And where are you going to plant seven hundred cedars?" she asked.

"On the open land at the back of the house."

"Kenju," said his elder brother, "you'd never get cedars to grow there. Why don't you help us a bit with the rice field instead?"

Kenju fidgeted uncomfortably and looked down at the ground.

But just then Kenju's father straightened up, wiping the sweat off his face. "Buy them for him, buy them," he said. "Why, he's never asked us to buy a single thing for him before. Let him have them."

Kenju's mother smiled as though relieved.

Full of joy, Kenju ran straight off in the direction of the house. He got an iron-headed hoe out of the barn and began earnestly turning up the turf to make holes for planting the cedars.

His elder brother, who had come after him, saw what he was doing and said: "Kenju, you have to dig deeper when you plant cedars. Wait till tomorrow. I'll go and buy the seedlings for you."

Unhappily, Kenju laid down the hoe.

The next day the sky was clear, the snow on the mountains shone pure white, and the larks chirped merrily as they soared up and up into the sky. And Kenju, grinning as though he could scarcely repress his joy, started digging holes for the seedlings just as his brother told him, beginning at the northern edge of the land. He dug them in absolutely straight

87

rows and at absolutely regular intervals. His elder brother planted one seedling in each hole in turn.

At this point, Heiji, who owned a field to the north of the piece of open ground, came along. He had a pipe in his mouth, and his hands were tucked inside his clothes, and his shoulders hunched up as though he was cold. Heiji did a little farming, but in reality he made a good part of his living in other, not so pleasant ways. "Hey, Kenju!" he called. "You really are stupid, aren't you, to plant cedars in a place like this. In the first place, they'll shut off the sunlight from my field."

Kenju turned red and looked as though he wanted to say something but couldn't get it out. He just stood there fidgeting helplessly.

So Kenju's elder brother, who was working a little way off, said: "Good morning, Heiji." He stood up, and Heiji ambled off again, muttering to himself as he went.

Nor was it Heiji alone who poked fun at Kenju for planting cedars on that stretch of grassy land. Everybody said the same things: no cedars would grow in a place like that; there was hard clay underneath; a fool was always a fool, after all.

And they were quite right. For the first five years, the green saplings grew straight up towards the sky, but from then on their heads grew round and in both the seventh and eighth years their height stayed at around nine feet.

One morning, as Kenju was standing in front of the grove, a farmer came along to have some fun with him. "Hey, Kenju. Aren't you going to prune those trees of yours?"

"Prune? What do you mean?"

"Pruning means cutting off all the lower branches with a hatchet."

"Then I think I'll prune them!"

Kenju ran and fetched a hatchet. Then he set about mercilessly lopping off the lower branches of the cedars. But

88

since the trees were, after all, only nine feet high, he had to stoop somewhat in order to get underneath them.

By dusk, every tree had been stripped of all its branches save for three or four at the very top. The grass below was covered with a layer of dark green branches, and the tiny wood lay bright and open. All of a sudden it had become so empty that Kenju was upset and felt almost guilty.

Kenju's elder brother, who came back just then from working in the fields, could not help smiling when he saw the wood. Then he said good-naturedly to Kenju, who was standing there looking blank: "Come on, let's gather the branches. We've got the stuff for a fine fire here. And the wood looks much better now, too."

This made Kenju feel easier at last, and together with his brother he went in under the trees and collected together all the branches that he had cut off. The grass beneath the trees was short and neat; it looked like the kind of place where you might well find two hermits playing chess.

But the next day, as Kenju was picking the worm-eaten beans out of the store in the barn, he heard a fearful clamor over in his wood. From all directions came voices giving orders, voices imitating bugles, feet stamping the ground, then suddenly a great burst of laughter that sent all the birds of the neighborhood flying up into the air. Startled, Kenju went to see what was going on.

And there, to his astonishment, he found a good fifty children on their way home from school, all drawn up in a line and marching in step between the rows of trees. Whichever way one went, of course, the rows of trees formed an avenue. And the trees themselves, in their green costumes, looked as though they too were marching in lines, which delighted the children still more. They were parading up and down between the trees with flushed faces, calling to each other as shrilly as a flock of shrikes.

In no time at all the rows of trees had been given names—Tokyo Street, Russia Street, Western Street. . . . Kenju was delighted. Watching from behind a tree, he opened his mouth wide and laughed out loud.

From then on, the children gathered there every day. The only times they did not come were when it was raining. On those days, Kenju would stand alone outside the grove, drenched to the skin in the rain that rustled down from the soft white sky.

"On guard at the wood again, Kenju?" people would say with a smile as they went by in their straw raincoats.

There were brown cones on the cedars, and from the tips of the fine green branches cold, crystal-clear drops of rain came splashing down. With his mouth wide open, Kenju laughed great breaths of laughter, standing there on and on, never tiring, while the steam rose from his small body in the rain.

One misty morning, though, Kenju suddenly bumped into Heiji in the place where people gathered rushes for thatching. Heiji looked carefully all around, then shouted at Kenju with an unpleasant, wolflike expression.

"Kenju! Cut your trees down!"

"Why?"

"Because they shut off the light from my field."

Kenju looked down at the ground without saying anything. At the most, the shadow of the cedars did not extend more than six inches into Heiji's field. What was more, the trees actually protected it from the strong south winds.

"Cut them down! Cut them down! You won't?"

"No! I won't," said Kenju rather fearfully, lifting his head. His lips were tense as though he might burst into tears at any moment. It was the only time in his whole life that he had ever said anything in defiance of another.

But Heiji, who felt annoyed at being snubbed by someone

as easygoing as Kenju, suddenly flew into a rage and, squaring his shoulders, began without warning to strike Kenju across the face. He struck him heavily, again and again.

Kenju let himself be struck in silence, with one hand held against his cheek, but before long everything about him went dark and he began to stagger. At this even Heiji must have begun to feel uncomfortable, for he hastily folded his arms and stalked off into the mist.

That autumn, Kenju died of typhus. Heiji too had died of the same sickness only ten days before. Yet every day the children gathered in the wood just as before, quite unconcerned about such matters.

The next year, the railway reached the village, and a station was built a mile or so from Kenju's house. Here and there, great china factories and silk mills sprang up. In time, the fields and paddies all about were eaten up by houses. Almost before people realized it, the village had become a full-fledged town. Yet by some chance Kenju's wood was the one thing that remained untouched. The trees, moreover, were still barely ten feet high, and still the children gathered there every day. Since a primary school had been built right close by, they gradually came to feel that the wood and the stretch of turf to the south of the wood were an extension of their own playground.

By now, Kenju's father was quite white-haired. And well he might be, for already it was close to twenty years since Kenju had died.

One day a young scholar, who had been born in what was then the village and was now a professor in some university in America, came to visit his old home for the first time in fifteen years. Yet look as he might, he could find no trace of the old fields and forests. Even the people of the town were mostly newcomers from other parts.

Then, one day, the professor was asked by the primary school to come and give a talk about foreign countries in the school hall. When the talk was over, the professor went out into the playground with the principal and the other teachers, and then walked together with them in the direction of Kenju's wood.

Suddenly, the young professor stopped in surprise and adjusted his spectacles repeatedly as though he doubted what he saw. Then at last he said, almost as though to himself: "Why, this is absolutely as it used to be! Even the trees are just as they always were. If anything, they seem to have got smaller. And the children are playing there. Why, I almost feel I might find myself and my old friends among them."

92

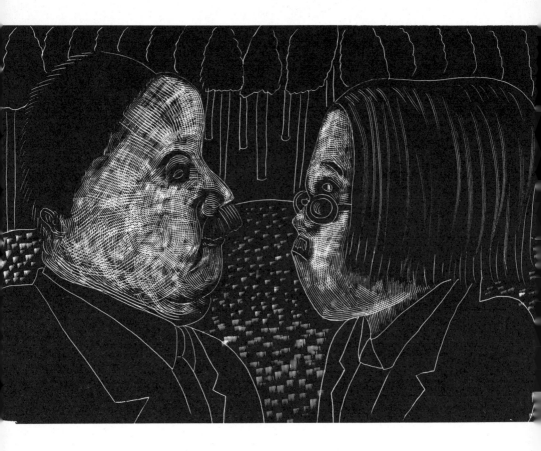

Then abruptly he smiled, as though suddenly recalling where he was, and said to the principal: "Is this a part of the school playground now?"

"No, the land belongs to the house over there, but they leave it for the children to play on just as they please. So in practice it's become a kind of additional playground for the school, even though it's not really ours."

"That's rather remarkable, isn't it? I wonder why it should be?"

"Ever since this place became built up everybody's been urging them to sell, but the old man, it seems, says it's the only thing he has to remember Kenju by, and that however hard up he is he will never let it go."

"Yes, yes—I remember. We used to think that Kenju was a bit wanting up top. He was forever laughing in a breathy kind of way. He used to stand just here every day and watch us children playing. They say it was he who planted all these trees. Ah me, who's to say who is wise and who is foolish? All one can say is that fate works in wondrous ways. This will always be a beautiful park for the children. How about it—how would it be if you called it the 'Kenju Wood' and kept it this way forever?"

"Now, that's a splendid idea! How happy the children would be!"

And so that was how it happened.

Right in the center of the grass in front of the children's wood, they set up an olive-colored slab of rock inscribed with the words "Kenju Wood."

Many letters and much money poured in to the school from attorneys and army officers and people with their own small farms in lands across the seas, all of whom had once been pupils at the school.

Kenju's family cried, they were so overjoyed.

Who can tell how many thousands of people learned what true happiness was, thanks to the cedar trees of the Kenju Wood, with their splendid dark green, their fresh scent, their cool shade in summer, and the turf with the color of moonlight that lay beneath.

And when it rained, the trees would drip great, cold, crystal-clear drops onto the turf below, and when the sun shone they would breathe out clean, new air all about them, just as they had done when Kenju himself was there.

Translated by John Bester
Illustrated by Osamu Tsukasa

Chasing Sparrows

by O Yong-su

Editors' Note. The original title of this story, meaning "adolescence," has been changed to avoid a certain ambiguity.

That afternoon so long ago had seemingly been quite forgotten. And yet it stayed somewhere deep in his memory, and one day it was recalled with vivid meaning, just as a seed buried in the earth suddenly bursts forth into the spring air after a long wait.

The boy Ung-a liked the housemaid best of all. Her name was Son-i, and she was soft and tender. He liked her more than he liked his mother and father, who were always busy with the farm work, or his grandmother, who was always weaving or spinning.

Son-i would scrape the scorched beans from the bottom of the iron pot and give them to him. Or when she was building a fire under the pot she would, according to the season, put some potatoes or an ear of corn or some sweet potatoes to roast in the ashes for him.

He couldn't say exactly when it was, but he remembered once he had dreamed he was sitting on the chamber pot, and when he woke he found his clothes were wet. His mother spanked him until there were red stripes on his buttocks. The she made him put a fan on his head and go beg salt from the neighbors to show that he had wet the bed. But Son-i hid him in a sunny place behind a huge pickle jar and, after drying his clothes before the fire, helped him dress.

Another time, just after the rainy season, he lost one of his rubber shoes while he was playing in the stream. His father, who had been raking the manure heap nearby, yelled for him to get out of the stream and told him he couldn't have any supper that night. And his mother came rushing out of the kitchen waving a straw broom over her head. Ung-a ran and hid in Son-i's skirts. Son-i managed to shield him from the broom, but in doing so she herself was struck savagely a couple of times.

Son-i usually took him with her wherever she went. But he noticed that she didn't offer to take him when she had just washed her hair or was wearing a new dress. When they were out together Son-i would carry him on her back even though it made people laugh to see such a big boy being carried piggyback.

Son-i used to take Ung-a with her when she went to wash clothes in the brook. In the summertime she would put him on the washing stone and carefully rub away the dirt from his neck, back, and groin. Ung-a protested that he was ticklish, but she kept on scrubbing his groin for a long, long time.

Nobody knew how long she had been doing it, but Son-i used to hide her face cream and powder in the haystack in the back yard, and nobody knew this except Ung-a. Whenever she was going on an errand or to a show, Son-i would hide behind the haystack and rub the cream into her face and then cover it with powder. Ung-a would stand guard for her to warn her if anyone was coming.

On this particular day, not long after the midautumn festival, Son-i took Ung-a with her to chase sparrows away from the rice field. There used to be huge flocks of sparrows in their village, and the birds would eat all the rice if they weren't kept away.

"Ung-a, whom do you like best?" Son-i asked as they

97

picked their way among tangles of soybean plants in the zigzag footpaths between rice paddies.

"I like Son-i best."

Laughing, Son-i knelt down and took the boy on her back. Then she said: "And if you were a rich man, Ung-a, to whom would you give most of your money."

"To Son-i! To Son-i!"

"And I like Ung-a more than anyone," Son-i said, holding him tighter against her back.

It was just past noon and there weren't many sparrows in

the millet field. The sun seemed hot enough to pop the grains of rice right out of their husks. Son-i didn't seem very interested in chasing sparrows anyway. Instead she brought out from under her skirt a pair of tight stockings. Her face cream and powder were inside the stockings. Son-i washed her face in water from the paddy and covered it with cream and powder. Then, after putting on the stockings, she let Ung-a climb on her back again and said they'd go see if the early-season beans and corn were ripe yet.

Their vegetable patch was on a nearby slope. Corn was

planted sparsely between the bean rows. Son-i seemed tired out and short of breath from climbing the steep slope. But she kept on climbing fast, hitching the boy up higher on her back from time to time and holding him tight. Sweat streamed along her ears onto her face and washed away the powder.

And suddenly, without their realizing it, there was Yon-ki's brother waiting for Son-i.

"Many sparrows?" Yon-ki's brother asked as he rolled a cigarette and lit it.

"When did you learn to smoke?" Son-i asked, her eyes wide with surprise.

Yon-ki's brother didn't answer at first but just grinned and kept on puffing at his cigarette. "What's wrong with my smoking? Do you think I'm a child still?"

"And what are you if you aren't a child?"

"Phooey!" Then he threw away his cigarette butt and, lifting Ung-a off the girl's back, sat him down on the A-frame he'd put down at the beginning of the bean patch. He began making a pair of spectacles out of corn shucks and an old piece of wire, while Son-i busied herself catching locusts and threading them on a string.

Son-i gave the string of threaded locusts to Ung-a and then walked away into the strip of millet, saying she was going to find some stalks of sweet corn for Ung-a to chew. Yon-ki's brother put the corn-shuck spectacles on Ung-a's nose, catching them behind his ears, and then he turned and followed Son-i.

Sitting on the A-frame, wearing the corn-shuck spectacles and holding the string of locusts in one hand, Ung-a had nothing to do but wait patiently for Son-i to come back with the cornstalks. But Son-i didn't come back and didn't come back. A hot-pepper fly began circling around Ung-a's head, and thinking of the sweet taste of young cornstalks, he became very hungry.

100

"Sister Son-i," he called out.

There was no answer.

"Son-i-ya, Son-i-ya. . . ." He kept calling and soon there were sobs in his voice. A little while later he began to cry in earnest.

After wailing a while he remembered the spectacles and felt to see if they were still on his nose. The locusts kept kicking and jerking, working their way slowly up the string. every once in a while he would push them back down, and he kept wailing into the emptiness.

Clouds were floating slowly across the sky. Swallows were darting and diving between the clouds like flying specks. He thought one cloud looked just like a horse. The more he looked at it, the more it seemed so. How splendid, he thought, if he too could fly on the cloud. Then he suddenly remembered the spectacles and felt for them again. And again he resumed his cries: "Son-i-ya!"

A cricket chirped in a bush beside him. He thought it was imitating his cries. And he called louder than ever: 'Son-i-ya!"

"Son-i-ya," chirped the cricket.

Ung-a was annoyed by the cricket. "You're a good-for-nothing little bug!" he called.

Getting up off the A-frame he went to the bush where he thought he could hear the cricket chirping. Very quietly, he looked and looked but he could not see the cricket. Then he began searching still more closely, looking hard at each bush, each twig. Yes, there it was, stealthily circling a branch of mugwort. It was larger than a grasshopper, with a pot belly and a hornlike tail. It was a cricket, sure enough.

Ung-a cupped his palm and, with a quick movement, had the cricket imprisoned in his hand. The cricket's desperate kicks hurt his hand. Cautiously, Ung-a opened his little finger and then the next finger, wanting a better look at the

101

cricket. Suddenly the cricket bit one of his fingers. Ung-a was surprised and opened his hand quickly, and the cricket disappeared with a single bound. Looking at his hand, Ung-a saw that his palm was stained with a drop of black, inklike saliva, and there were two red specks at the tip of one finger, as if made by a needle.

Sitting down again on the A-frame, Ung-a began crying as he looked at the red specks on his finger. The more he looked, the more it hurt. He kept on crying, looking at his finger from time to time through tear-filled eyes, and each time he looked, he started crying again with doubled force, helplessly. Then he would check to make sure the spectacles were still there and keep pushing the locusts back down on their string.

A hawk came flying overhead and circled twice over the millet field. The ears of millet began to stir and then rippling waves came toward him among the millet plants.

"Ung-a dear." It was Son-i, who had returned to him at last. Her cheeks were apple red, and she seemed especially pretty to him at this moment. Her eyelids looked soft and creamy.

"What's the matter, Ung-a? Why are you crying?"

Ung-a wiped the tears from his eyes and held up his finger for her to see.

"What's the matter?"

"The cricket—it bit me!"

Son-i blew her warm breath on the red specks and then turned her back for him to climb on. She said the corn wasn't ripe yet, so she hadn't brought him any stalks to chew. Then, making no more attempt to chase the sparrows away, she started for home, taking a shortcut.

"Whom do you like best, Ung-a dear?" she asked over her shoulder.

"Son-i, I like Son-i best."

102

She held him tighter against her back. "And where have you been this afternoon?"

"To the fields to chase the sparrows away."

"With whom?"

"With Son-i and Yon-ki's brother."

Son-i stopped. "No, you mustn't say that. You went just with Son-i. Isn't that so?"

"But Yon-ki's brother was there too."

"No, no. You hate Yon-ki's brother. You wouldn't have gone with him because you hate him. Isn't that so?"

"But didn't he make spectacles for me?"

"No, you hate him. I hate him. You hate him too, huh?"

The boy was silent.

"Yon-ki's brother wasn't there, huh?"

Still he said nothing.

Son-i set him down on the footpath between two rice paddies. "Then I won't carry you on my back. And from now on I won't give you anything either," she said, glaring at him. She jerked the spectacles off his nose and tore them to pieces.

Unga-a could not understand why she was being so mean to him and he felt sad. He was tearful and helpless because he could not understand why she was so angry.

Son-i turned away from him and walked on toward home, leaving him to follow. Several times she glared back at him over her shoulder.

They walked on in silence. Suddenly she stopped and knelt down to wipe the tears from his eyes with the hem of her skirt. Then she offered her back to him again.

As he was climbing on, she said: "You hate Yon-ki's brother. Isn't that so?"

"Yes."

"You hate him. He wasn't with us today. Isn't that so?"

"Yes."

104

"You went to the fields just with Son-i. Isn't that so?"

"Yes, yes."

"I like Ung-a best of all."

"I like Son-i best too." As he spoke, he picked some dry grass out of Son-i's hair.

That night in bed Ung-a thought about the corn-shuck spectacles, and he wondered about Yon-ki's brother's A-frame, which had been left lying by the millet field. By the next morning, however, he had forgotten all about everything. It would be many long years before he remembered again.

Translated by Kim Dae-yon
Illustrated by Kim Young-ju

MALAYSIA

The Red Pencil

by Ali Majid

Editors' Note. This story has been abridged by omitting a few episodes concerning the adult characters.

After recess, Mr. Jamal approached the classroom doors. The students saw him coming, ran back to their seats, and sat down quietly. The room was completely silent.

Mr. Jamal paused at the door. He looked to see that all was in order, then stepped slowly into the room. His footsteps sounded loudly in the silence. The children constantly stole glances at their teacher's shiny black shoes.

"Rise!" called the class monitor.

All the students stood up. Some stood sideways, some leaning forward, some stood on one leg, a few were half sitting, half standing, while others still munched on the remainders of their cakes.

"May peace be with you, sir," came the thunderous chorus from all thirty-five students at once.

"And with you. Be seated. Take out your geography books."

The room was hot. So many children in such a small room made it even hotter. Mr. Jamal approached his desk, wiping the sweat from his face, and sat down. Seeing that the teacher was seated, the class monitor walked up to him and said: "During the recess just now, there were some students fighting."

"Who? Pupils from which class?" Mr. Jamal asked anxiously. It was Wednesday, the day Mr. Jamal was on duty. He was responsible for anything that happened that day.

"Our class, sir," replied the class monitor.

"Who was it?"

"Zahid and Dolah."

All the students in the classroom turned to look at Zahid and Dolah. Then they looked back at Mr. Jamal. From the corner of the room came the sound of stifled sobs. The students again turned toward the corner and saw that Dolah was crying.

"Zahid! Dolah! Come here," the teacher commanded in a threatening voice. The students could recognize any change in the tone of their teacher's voice and knew just what it meant.

The two guilty pupils stepped forward. They were scared and uncomfortable. Dolah dragged along behind Zahid, crying even more.

"Why did you fight?"

Neither of them answered. Only Dolah's sobs could be heard. The other children watched closely and did not make a sound.

"Why were you fighting?" the teacher asked again.

"Dolah stole my pencil, sir," Zahid reported.

"No sir, he said that my pencil was his," put in Dolah.

"Whose pencil is it actually?"

"Mine, sir," replied Zahid quickly.

"Mine, sir," said Dolah right after.

"Dolah, go get that pencil and bring it here," said Mr. Jamal.

Dolah went quickly to his desk. He rummaged in his bag, found the pencil, and returned to the front of the room. He had stopped crying.

Mr. Jamal held the pencil in his hand. He stared at the pencil trying to think of a way to solve the problem.

"Now, what makes you think that this pencil belongs to you?"

"There's a mark on it made by a knife, sir," said Dolah boldly.

"You, Zahid?"

"Er, there's a mark on it made by a knife, sir."

"He's lying, sir."

"What letter did you carve on the pencil, Zahid?"

"Er. . . ." He shook his head.

"What about you, Dolah?"

"The letter D, sir. That's the first letter of my name."

"Correct. So this pencil belongs to Dolah. Zahid made three mistakes: stealing, lying, and fighting. His prize is three strokes from the cane."

Zahid received the strokes from the teacher. His face turned bright red and he stared round-eyed at Mr. Jamal. Then he returned to his desk. He looked very sad and the tears trickled down his face.

Mr. Jamal was proud that he had been able to settle the fight fairly. He began the next lesson as usual. After the students had settled down to written exercises, Mr. Jamal sat back in his chair and relaxed. He took the opportunity to read.

When Mr. Jamal was engrossed in his book, Zahid quietly slid over to where Dolah was sitting. He stared at his enemy fiercely.

"You liar."

"Ha, ha. You got three strokes."

"You took my pencil. You made that sign on it yourself, then claimed it was yours. Very clever."

Zahid punched Dolah in the shoulder. Dolah fell back in his chair. He started yelling and Zahid quickly slid back to his seat.

"What's this?" Mr. Jamal looked up from his book. Then

he banged the book down on his desk and stared at the two boys.

"Zahid hit me, sir," Dolah told the teacher.

Mr. Jamal called Zahid to come to the front of the class. Zahid walked forward slowly.

"What did you do?"

"He took my pencil and. . . ."

"I asked you what you were doing just now."

"Nothing. He took my pencil, then. . . ."

"No, no. I didn't ask you that. What I asked was what you did just now. Understand?"

He slapped Zahid's cap. Dust flew into the air and the cap covered Zahid's eyes and nose.

"Wasn't it you who punched Dolah just now?"

Zahid was silent. He stared hard into Mr. Jamal's face.

"Yes or no?" Mr. Jamal almost shouted.

Zahid shifted uncomfortably. His face was sullen.

"He took my pencil; then he scraped off the paint and made that mark."

"I've told you I'm not accusing you of taking that pencil. You'd better confess you hit Dolah."

The boy was quiet. Only his eyes blinked like a sickened lizard after eating limes. His face showed no emotion.

"Confess, stupid!"

But Zahid kept silent and stood like an old tree, rooted to the spot. He showed no reaction to Mr. Jamal's shouting.

"All right, now. Confess! Confess!"

Mr. Jamal pulled Zahid's ear. The other children looked up from their books. They wanted to watch the drama between the teacher and Zahid.

"I hit Dolah," Zahid admitted. His voice was weak. He felt as though he had been cheated. Dolah smiled triumphantly.

"Ha! That's better. Are you going to do it again?"

Mr. Jamal pinched and pulled Zahid's arms. Zahid had to stand on his toes, trying to keep his balance. His face and ears reddened in pain and embarrassment.

"No," he said in a hollow voice. It was a sign that he had lost.

On his way back to his desk, he stared at Dolah. His teeth were clenched. He could not take it any longer. He felt like strangling Dolah there and then. Zahid could not bear seeing the thief who stole his pencil, safe and sound. Moreover the thief had the teacher on his side.

Zahid liked his pencil so much because he had gotten it on his own initiative. The pencil was very special. Its length was double that of an ordinary pencil and it was a beautiful red color. At one end there was a plastic hook. The eraser, which could be detached from the hook, was exceptionally large too.

The first time he had seen the pencil hanging in the shop,

he had liked it. He had wanted to own that special pencil. On his way home he had imagined how proud he would be if the pencil were his.

"It would last longer than a year's worth of writing," he had whispered to himself.

Whenever Mr. Jamal asked questions in class, Zahid was unable to make his raised hand seen. He felt miserable because he could not show his abilities. But he did not blame his teacher.

"I'm too small," he said to himself. "Nobody ever sees me."

But if he had that pencil, maybe it would help him. He would raise the pencil high and catch Mr. Jamal's attention. Then he would be called on. Also, the eraser was large enough to lend to his friends. He would not mind if they borrowed it. It would make him proud. But how much was the pencil? He ran back to the store to check the price.

"Hey, how much is this pencil?" he asked the shopkeeper.

"It's cheap. Only fifty cents."

Zahid shrugged his shoulders. He had only ten cents. But he did not lose hope—his grandmother might have some money. He ran home and told his grandmother that he wanted to buy that pencil.

"Don't you have a pencil, Zahid?"

"It's too short, Grandma."

"There's nothing wrong with a short pencil. We're not rich people."

"The teacher is always complaining that my pencil is as short as the hair in his nose."

His grandmother had only two dollars. There would be a Parents' Day at the school, and the two dollars had to be saved for that special day.

"I have an idea, Zahid. There's a holiday the day after tomorrow, isn't there?"

"Yes, Grandma, I don't have to go to school."

"You go and follow your uncle when he taps rubber on the plantation. You can collect the rubber scraps."

Zahid agreed. If he got more than fifty cents, he would try to buy a ruler too. His old ruler was as jagged as a saw blade.

At last the pencil came into his possession. The first time he held it in his hand, he trembled, he was so happy. He smiled and felt like telling everybody about his extraordinary pencil. At school he showed his new pencil proudly to his friends. Some of them shared his happiness, while others could not help feeling a bit envious.

A few days later the pencil was missing. Zahid became very gloomy. He told all of his friends, but they could not cheer him up. And the very next day he saw Dolah writing with a long pencil. The length of the pencil was exactly the same as the one he had lost. But Dolah's pencil looked a bit strange. Its red paint had been scraped off.

"Where did you get that pencil, Dolah?" Zahid asked.

113

"My father bought it for me yesterday."

"Why did you scrape the paint off?"

"Don't want it to be the same as yours."

"I've lost mine."

"That's why I scraped the paint off. Otherwise, you'd accuse me of stealing."

"Let me see it."

"No, you can't."

"I see the eraser has already been used."

"I used it."

"You used it that much?"

"I used it a lot last night."

"That's my pencil. I recognize it."

"No, it's not. My father bought it for me."

"How much was it, then?"

"How do I know?"

"He would have told you."

"I don't know."

"If your father really bought it, then you must have asked him the price."

"That's enough." Dolah tried to get away, but Zahid stopped him.

"One more thing, if it was bought only yesterday, why is it so short?"

Dolah did not answer. He wanted to run away, but Zahid was holding tightly onto his shoulder.

"You stole my pencil!" yelled Zahid.

"No!"

"Yes! Yes! This is my pencil!"

Zahid tried to snatch the pencil away. Dolah pushed him and he fell on the ground. Zahid got up again quickly and they began to fight. The other children crowded around in a circle, shouting and encouraging the two fighters. Zahid lost the fight. He was smaller than Dolah. And now he had lost again in class since Mr. Jamal believed Dolah and punished Zahid.

The bell rang, announcing the end of the day. Zahid ran out of the room. Mr. Jamal tried to call him back, but he paid no attention. He banged the door loudly as he left, letting off steam. Mr. Jamal shouted at him again. Zahid continued to ignore his teacher. He knocked over a flower pot at the foot of the steps. The pot broke and he took off like a wild horse.

He stopped at a crossroads. Then, looking to the right and the left, he crept into the undergrowth nearby and waited for Dolah. At last Dolah walked by and Zahid leapt from

his hiding place like a hungry tiger. Dolah fell down and
Zahid hit him in the stomach and then on the chin.

Their friends tried to pull them apart but failed. Zahid
fought with all his strength. His face became black and blue.

He was bleeding. But he won. Zahid opened Dolah's bag,
found the pencil, broke it in pieces, and hurled the pieces
into the river. Then he ran home.

After he got home, he looked for his grandmother. When
he found her, he hugged her and put his head in her lap.
Then he cried his heart out.

That night Zahid got sick. In his sleep, he often cried out
about his pencil. His grandmother looked after him all night.

The fever lasted for three days. He lost weight and seemed to be even smaller.

When he felt better, he went back to school. But now Zahid was no longer the quiet Zahid of the days before the incident. He had changed. Nearly every five minutes, Mr. Jamal's students could be heard calling out: "Sir, look at Zahid. He is disturbing me. Sir, Zahid is pulling my hair. Sir, Zahid splashed ink on my nose. Sir, Zahid hit me." All the time it was Zahid.

"Zahid. Go back to your seat," ordered Mr. Jamal.

Mr. Jamal could not endure all the trouble Zahid was causing. When he could stand it no longer, he would call Zahid out of the room.

"You've become a great nuisance now, eh?"

Zahid just raised his eyebrows. He looked through the teacher as if nothing had happened. He even seemed amused.

"If you don't have a book or a pencil you can just go home. Here you're just a nuisance. A menace."

The teacher's insults had no effect on him. Zahid's face remained calm and showed no emotion. Sometimes he even stared right into Mr. Jamal's eyes as if he wanted to challenge him to a duel.

"Stand there until it's time to go home," Mr. Jamal commanded.

Zahid stood in a corner of the room. But Zahid only looked amused; a smile played on his lips. This made Mr. Jamal angrier than ever.

One day, on his way home, Dolah was waiting for him. Luckily, Zahid had a stick with him.

"Don't come near me, Dolah. I'll hit you."

Zahid swung the stick in Dolah's face. Dolah dared not come near. But Dolah did not lose hope. He looked for a stick too. Seeing that Dolah might find a stick at any minute, Zahid ran home as fast as his legs could carry him.

That night he asked his grandmother for some money. He said he wanted to buy a book. But when he reached the bookstore, he saw the red pencil and suddenly felt very sad. He decided he did not need the book after all. Then he saw a penknife in the showcase and bought it instead.

The knife would save him from Dolah. And maybe he could do even more with the help of the penknife. He sharpened the knife carefully.

From then on, he went to school with no intention of learning. He liked to disturb the other students and keep them from learning. He poured oil into the fishbowl in the science corner. He pulled up the beanstalks and ferns. He destroyed the insect collections. Now he felt satisfied and free.

He was always punished for the trouble he made. Zahid bravely accepted any punishment. Sometimes Zahid's bravery made Mr. Jamal unsure of himself. It was as if the punishment had no effect. Whenever he was punished, his hand would feel for the penknife in his pocket. It was as though the penknife gave him the strength he needed.

After being punished, he was ordered back to his desk. He showed his defiance by stabbing the desk with his knife. The penknife stood erect and shook violently. To Zahid, the knife was sticking into Mr. Jamal's chest. He smiled. Mr. Jamal saw what Zahid had done, but he pretended to look elsewhere.

One day Zahid hurt Dolah with the penknife. This was a serious case, so Zahid and Dolah were brought before the headmaster. Mr. Jamal suggested that Zahid be sent to a reform school. Dolah was allowed to return to class, but Zahid was kept to talk with the headmaster.

The headmaster took a long look at Zahid. All the reports made by Mr. Jamal came back to his mind. He had slammed the door, broken the flower pot, fought, disturbed the other students, had not been eager to learn, and now he had hurt

118

Dolah with a penknife. But the peculiar thing was that Zahid had been known as a quiet and well-mannered pupil previously.

The headmaster cleared his throat. He tried to find some suitable words to begin his conversation with Zahid. Then he pretended to look for a knife to sharpen his pencil.

"Do you have a knife, Zahid?" he asked with a smile.

Zahid shook his head.

"If you have one, please lend it to me. My pencil is blunt."

Zahid did not know what to do. He was afraid of the headmaster. As if forced to do so, he put his hand into his pocket and drew out the knife. He handed it to the headmaster, who took it with a smile.

"Your knife is very sharp, isn't it, Zahid?"

Zahid nodded.

"Why do you need such a sharp knife?"

"Er, Dolah. . . ." He shook his head.

"Are you angry with Dolah?"

"Yes."

"Are you afraid of him?"

"Yes."

"What did Dolah do to you?"

"He stole my pencil. Then. . . ."

Zahid was overcome with emotion. He started to cry. He remembered the pencil that he had liked so much, that Dolah had stolen from him. He remembered how he had had to destroy it with his own hands.

The headmaster spoke softly like Zahid's own grandmother. His grandmother was kind, so the headmaster must be kind too. All these thoughts made him cry even harder.

"Zahid, I'll look into this case again. If Dolah is in the wrong, what do you want to do to him?"

"Nothing, sir. I only want Mr. Jamal to know that the pencil was mine, and not Dolah's," he replied between sobs.

"All right. Now you can go back to your class."

After Zahid was gone, the headmaster went to see Mr. Jamal. Then Zahid and Dolah were brought in front of the headmaster and closely questioned again. Dolah finally admitted everything about stealing the pencil.

The headmaster spoke to Mr. Jamal in a low voice: "When you gave him the beating, it was for no wrong that he had done. And I think that made Zahid think of his father. Maybe you didn't know: Zahid's father is a cruel man. Maybe Zahid saw the father he hates in you." Then turning to Zahid, he said: "We're sorry we didn't understand what really happened. I'm going to buy another pencil just like your old one and give it to you."

At these words, Mr. Jamal smiled and nodded, and Dolah looked more sheepish than ever. As for Zahid, he could not tell how he really felt: happy, sad, or simply grateful. All of these feelings mingled in his heart. Already he could feel the new red pencil in his hands.

Translated by Hamidah Abdul Hamid
Illustrated by Ariff Mohamad

Maya and Her Kid

by Ramesh Bikal

In the foothills of our majestic Himalayas there is a certain small village. It has some eight or ten houses surrounded with green trees and bushes. Among the houses in that village you will see a tiny house. It is whitewashed, colored with red clay on the lower part, and roofed with yellow straw. That is Maya's house—Maya the little village girl.

Maya is a very beautiful girl. She is about ten years old. She lives in the house with her parents and her two pets— Khaire, a brown dog, and Tilkane, a little, restless black goat. The goat is called Tilkane because she has white spots on her

ears and Tilkane means white spots. But Maya usually calls
her Mune, which means little kid.

Mune is a very naughtly and mischievous kid. Maya wants
her to be quiet and gentle, but she seldom obeys Maya.
She strays off and Maya does not like it. So she has built
a small pen where she can keep Mune when she is away
from the house. Maya is afraid that Mune's naughtiness may
lead her into real danger someday. She is worried about the
cunning jackal that killed another kid in the village the week
before. Now he is waiting for a chance to catch Maya's kid
too. Maya has to take good care of Mune so the wicked jackal
will not kill her.

But that naughty kid just would not pay attention to
Maya's warnings. No sooner would Maya go out of sight
than Mune would somehow get out of the pen. Then Mune
would wander all around the village making trouble. She
would run here and there, jumping and dancing from ter-

122

race to terrace and from lane to lane. Sometimes she would go outside the village to graze. Mune enjoyed escaping from the entire village. Khaire the dog, obeying his kind mistress, would try to stop Mune and make her stay home, but she would not pay any attention. Poor Khaire could only stand by, watching the kid's dancing and jumping. When Maya came home from school, she often found that Mune had gotten into some trouble. Sometimes when she found that the kid had escaped from the pen, she would worry and begin to look for her, calling: "Mune, Mune. Here is something for you to eat." Poor Khaire would follow Maya, waving his tail. His eyes looked very guilty as if he thought he was responsible.

Despite all the trouble that Mune caused, Maya loved the little kid from the bottom of her heart. Mune and Khaire were the only things Maya could call her own and be proud of. So it was very important for her to take good care of them. Mune had been given to her by her parents on a special occasion. She loved her very much and could forgive her for anything.

Usually, when Maya came back from school she remembered to bring some green vegetables for Mune, not even being sure she would find her safely in her pen. When she did find Mune in the pen, she was very happy. Mune would come jumping and dancing to greet Maya. Maya would pick the little kid up and hug her and give her something good to eat. And if she ever found Mune a little sad, Maya would be very worried and begin asking Khaire: "Tell me, Khaire, what happened to that little kid?" But poor Khaire, what could he answer? All he could do was bark and wag his tail.

Then one day, before going to school, Maya fed Mune well and put her in her pen, saying to her: "Listen to me, you naughty girl. I'll put you into your pen now and go to school. I'll be back late this afternoon. Don't try to get out of your pen. When I come home I'll bring lots of greens for you to eat, all right?" Then she turned toward Khaire and ordered him to take good care of the little kid. "Look here, Khaire," she said, "you will be looking after Mune while I'm away. Don't let her get away and make trouble. Don't let her go far from home. Be careful of that wicked jackal, because if he finds Mune, that will really be the end of her."

After giving these orders to Khaire and Mune, Maya left for school. But just a little later, after she was out of sight, there was a strange noise from the other side of the village. When Khaire heard the noise, he could not help running toward it to find out what it was. He forgot everything Maya had told him and went running to the other side of the village barking loudly. This was a perfect opportunity for Mune and she did not want to lose it. She somehow managed to get out of the pen and ran here and there, jumping and dancing from terrace to terrace and from lane to lane. And at last, over-joyed to be free, she ran right out of the village.

At that very moment the wicked jackal was watching Mune's every move, looking for an opportunity to catch her. What better chance could he get than this? And besides, he was very hungry. Mune would be a good dinner for him. . . . He jumped out of his hiding place and stood right in front of that stupid little kid.

"Now, little one, after a long wait I've got you in the end!" The jackal laughed with joy and said: "Say a prayer if you can."

Mune now realized the danger before her. But who was to blame except herself? It was her own foolishness that had led her into this danger. She trembled with fear, thinking the jackal would eat her at any minute. She whimpered and begged the jackal for her life. "Pray, do not kill me, Mr. Jackal. I'm just a little kid, much too small to satisfy your big appetite."

124

"I know that you're just a kid and not enough to satisfy my big appetite," said the cunning jackal, "but I will be quite content with your meat. The meat of a small kid tastes much better than the meat of a large goat. I love tender meat more than anything else."

Mune prayed for her life again and again and asked the jackal to be kind, but all in vain. He grabbed her in his mouth and ran away into the jungle with her.

A little while later, Khaire the dog came home and found that Mune was missing. He was very worried about her. Instantly, he sensed a familiar smell in the air and understood at once what had happened to Mune. What he smelled was nothing other than the smell of that cunning jackal. "So!" he thought, "the jackal has caught Mune."

Now Khaire immediately decided to run after the jackal by following the strong smell. About five hundred yards away from the village there was a small jungle of overgrown bushes and trees. Khaire rushed into the jungle and found Mune and the jackal under a big yellow berry bush. Mune was trembling in great terror before the jackal, who was about to eat her up.

Khaire could not stand the sight and rushed violently

toward the cunning jackal, but that sly animal was smarter than Khaire. Before Khaire could catch him, he disappeared like lightning into the thick jungle bushes. Khaire chased the jackal a bit farther, but he could not get to him; so he returned to Mune.

He tried to lead Mune home, but she had already been hurt by the jackal's sharp teeth and couldn't move a single step. Khaire did not like to leave her in such a miserable condition. He remained beside Mune, guarding her faithfully.

In the evening, Maya came home and discovered that both Mune and Khaire were missing. She was very worried about them and began to look for them here and there. She ran from the house to the farm and from the farm to the house, but she could find no trace of them. Maya called: "Mune! Where have you gone? Mune! Come and eat."

She searched for them for a long time, but all in vain, and she became more and more worried. She asked everyone if they had seen Mune and Khaire. Where had they vanished to? Had the sky swallowed them up? No, they must be somewhere nearby. Maya decided to go into the jungle to look for them.

It was already getting dark when she arrived at the edge of the jungle. There was a curtain of twilight falling over the branches of the trees. The snow-covered peaks of the great Himalayas were shining with the golden rays of the setting sun. They looked as if they could be the golden roofs of the temples of heaven. At the same time, the chilly winter evening wind was beginning to blow and Maya began to shake with cold. But even this could not stop her and she kept going.

Then through the dim evening light she saw two small, black objects like lumps of stone. Her heart beat faster and she ran toward them and found her two lovely pets.

126

"You two little rascals, how could you disobey me?" Maya pretended to be angry, but she held the little kid tightly in her arms. Maya soon realized that Mune had been seriously hurt.

"Oh! my love, what happened to you? How did you get hurt? Who did it?" She was so upset that she almost started crying. Her hand touched the wound very gently. The wound seemed to cause pain in Maya's own heart too. She looked at Khaire as if she were asking: "How did it happen, Khaire?" Khaire simply waved his tail and tried to avoid Maya's eyes. Khaire felt it was all his fault. Mune, even in Maya's arms, looked scared. She was crying out and trembling with fear. Now Maya did not need any more explanation. She understood that Mune had somehow gotten out of her pen and the cunning jackal had found his opportunity to grab her.

128

"I understand what you mean by those cries, you naughty kid!" said Maya. "You are begging me to forgive you for not obeying me, aren't you? All right, I'll pardon you this time, but if you make the same mistake again, that rascal Mr. Jackal won't let you live any longer, understand?"

"Come on, Khaire, let's go home now. This Mune was punished quite enough for disobeying me. This time she was taught a good lesson. I'm glad she didn't have to pay too much for it. I'll have to do a great deal of nursing, though," Maya said and started walking home carrying Mune in her arms with Khaire following along behind.

Translated by Laxmi Shrestha
Illustrated by Tek Bir Mukhiya

PAKISTAN

And He Lived Forever After

by Mahmud Khawar

That night Saleem could hardly sleep. In his half dreams, half nightmares, he once again faced death, the calamity that had taken his father away five years ago. Saleem had been only six at the time.

As Saleem tossed restlessly on the bed, those painful memories came back to him. They were mixed up with what he had heard about the epidemic that had killed so many people in the village recently. He remembered how his father had returned suddenly from the military camp. He had looked very tired and ill. Soon after that, the doctor had told them that his father was going to die. All efforts to save his life had failed. A few days later, his father had died. Even after all these years, he could not forget that terrible night.

Until late that night, he had stayed beside his father's bed. When his eyes became heavy with sleep, his mother had sent him to bed. He has only a hazy recollection of what happened later. The night was dark and cold. The sky was filled with heavy clouds and a strong wind beat against the windows. He must have been sleeping soundly when he was disturbed by voices. His father was talking in a low voice.

"Don't cry, Tayyeba. I know my end has come. But I am not worried about it. What worries me is Saleem's future. He is so young. I want him to study and then join the army. I want him to grow up as an educated, brave young man. Tayyeba, please never allow him to do any menial work." Then he stopped talking, since he was very short of breath.

130

Saleem could not hear his mother's reply because she was weeping softly. Before he could get out of bed and go to them, he heard his mother scream. He jumped out of bed, rushed to her, and found that his father had died peacefully, leaving them to the care of Allah.

Saleem lived in a small town in the Punjab. It had a primary school up to the fifth grade. To look after the health of the people in that area, there was also a government hospital and several private clinics. Saleem was now in the fifth grade. He was well known in his school for his intelligence and good manners.

Most of the people in the town were farmers and traders. They were simple people and felt as if they belonged to one big family. Whenever they had a problem, they would all assemble at some central place in the town to try and find a good solution. That day, when Saleem was returning home from school, he saw a group of people standing in the shade of a huge tree. They all looked sad and worried.

"Allah have mercy on us! This is the fourth death today. And all are dying from the same mysterious disease. It must be the wrath of Allah," someone said, shaking his head gloomily.

"Brother, Allah is merciful and kind. He never punishes unjustly. What we are facing now is the result of our own misdeeds," the old man sitting nearby replied, scratching his head thoughtfully.

Saleem stopped for a while and listened to them. They were discussing the epidemic that was attacking the people in one area of the town, and the many deaths that were occurring. Thank God he lived in another part of town, far from the sickness.

The strange feeling that the shadow of death had fallen on the town made him shiver. He thought of his mother and how she had wept so much after the death of his father that she had gone blind within a year. Since then she had been in constant need of proper care and protection. They needed money and grain and all the other necessities of life. These came only from the one piece of land that they owned. And that land also needed proper care and hard work.

Although Saleem's ancestors had been farmers, he was too young and inexperienced to look after the land. Moreover, he was eager to follow in his father's footsteps and join the army to serve his country. So they had decided to lease the land to an honest elderly farmer, Ramzan Baba. He tilled it for them and, after each harvest, shared the grain with them.

Thus after his father's death, Saleem had to rely on Ramzan Baba for his family's living. That night, half awake and half sleeping, he thought of the kind old farmer and remembered the day the year before when he had visited Ramzan's house for the first time.

Ramzan Baba lived on the outskirts of town in a small house. Most of the people living in that area were farmers or laborers. Beyond the houses, spreading over several acres,

there were rows and rows of paddy fields. It was from these
very fields that hard-working farmers produced some of
Pakistan's best-quality rice.

In order to reach Ramzan Baba's house, one had to walk
quite a distance, crossing several parts of town and then
beautiful meadows. The house was neatly built with mud
walls and a thatch roof. Near its entrance there was a large
shade tree. To the right of the tree there was a covered pen
for the pair of sturdy brown bullocks and the buffalo, chewing
their cuds peacefully. There were also a few goats wandering
around.

Ramzan Baba greeted Saleem warmly. He took him inside
the house and introduced him to his three daughters. The
youngest, Aashu, was Saleem's age. Their mother had died
long ago and it was their father who had brought them up.
After the introductions, Saleem was offered a seat on the

133

charpoy bed on which Ramzan Baba had spread a clean bed sheet. Ramzan himself sat down on the other bed. For a while he and Ramzan Baba talked about the weather and the coming harvest. A few minutes later, Aashu came into the room with two large glasses of buttermilk. She offered one shyly to Saleem and gave the other to her father. Aashu was dressed in traditional clothing and had a charming and innocent face.

"You shouldn't have taken so much trouble for me, Sister Aashu," Saleem said. Aashu was glad that he had called her "sister" and smiled at him affectionately.

"Now that you have called her 'sister,' you shouldn't behave so formally. Drink the buttermilk. It's made from our Rani's milk, which is the best in town," Ramzan Baba declared proudly. Rani was the name of their buffalo.

That day, after resting a while, they went to Saleem's fields. Saleem found them in good shape. While explaining how he planned to sow the next crop, Ramzan Baba told Saleem about the serious water shortage. For the last two years, there had not been much rain and the farmers had been depending on the canal for water. The canal was several hundred yards away from the fields; so each farmer had dug an irrigation ditch to his field.

"Why don't we do it also?" asked Saleem.

"It's not a job for one man, Saleem. I am too old to do it alone," replied Ramzan Baba.

"Who asked you to do it alone? I'll join you," Saleem replied confidently.

"No, Saleem, this is a very difficult job, and besides, on his deathbed your father made your mother promise never to allow you to do menial labor."

"Oh, Ramzan Baba, working in one's own fields is not a menial job. After all, I am also from a family of farmers. These days I have plenty of time. Please don't stop me. We'll

134

dig the ditch together. We can start tomorrow," Saleem declared firmly.

That night as time ticked by and the moon began to lose its brightness, Saleem's restlessness disappeared. His dreams became more pleasant; he saw water flowing into his fields, which were filled with rice in full tassel. Soon he fell into a deep sleep.

The next day, Saleem returned from school as soon as his classes were over. He ate his lunch quickly and went straight to the fields. It was a fine day. The sun had just disappeared for a moment behind a large white cloud that looked like a huge lion's head. Ramzan Baba had not arrived yet; so Saleem sat down in the shade of a tree. It was so peaceful and quiet there. Suddenly he heard a noise, and turned to find Aashu coming toward him. He was surprised and got up to greet her.

"What are you doing here?" he asked abruptly.

"I am here to help you and my father," she replied and smiled.

"A girl can't help much," Saleem laughed.

"Don't laugh, Saleem. I know I can't dig, but at least I can clear the weeds after they are cut. Won't you let me help?" she pleaded.

Before Saleem could reply, Ramzan Baba appeared from behind a row of trees. He was carrying shovels and pickaxes. "Your suggestion is quite sensible, Aashu," Ramzan declared. "We will need someone to carry away the weeds and grass. Now come on, Saleem, let's get to work."

Saleem could not argue, but somehow he did not like the idea of Aashu working with them. Unwillingly, he picked up a sharp shovel and began cutting the bushes. For several hours they worked silently. By afternoon prayer time, a large part of the land was cleared.

From that day on, it became a routine for them to work after lunch time. On the seventh day, all of the bushes right up to the bank of the canal had been cut. Only a patch of grass and some weeds were left. Before cutting them, Saleem stopped to wipe the sweat from his face. Then he turned to see what Aashu was doing, and he saw something that froze the blood in his veins.

A large black snake was moving in the grass behind Aashu. It was close to her, but she was unaware of it. There was no time to warn her since that would startle the snake and make it bite her. So swift as lightning he rushed toward her and pushed her away from the hissing snake. Aashu fell, and Saleem also lost his balance, slipped, and fell on the snake.

Not knowing what was happening, Ramzan Baba looked at them in surprise. Just then he also saw the black snake under Saleem. With a cry of despair, Ramzan leaped forward and cut the snake in two with his shovel. He pulled Saleem away, but it was too late. The snake had already bitten Saleem on his thigh and he was moaning in pain.

They rushed him to a hospital. Everything humanly possible was done to save his life. But by the time Aashu brought Tayyeba, Saleem's mother, to the hospital, the young hero was dead. Aashu and Ramzan Baba knew that for them he could never die, but would live forever after in their hearts.

Translated by Anwar Enayatullah
Illustrated by Mohammad Wasim

137

Roosters and Hens

by Alejandro R. Roces

Editors' Note. This story comes from Philippine Contemporary Literature, *edited by Asuncion David-Maramba (Bookmark, 1970).*

My brother Kiko once had a very peculiar chicken. It was peculiar because no one could tell whether it was a rooster or a hen. My brother claimed it was a rooster. I said it was a hen. We got into a lot of trouble trying to settle the argument.

The whole thing began early one morning. Kiko and I were driving the chickens out of the cornfield. The corn had just been planted and the chickens were scratching the seeds out of the ground for food. Suddenly we heard a staccato flapping of wings. We turned toward it and saw two chickens fighting at the far end of the field. We couldn't see the birds clearly since they were lunging at each other in a cloud of feathers and dust.

"Just look at that rooster fight!" my brother exclaimed, pointing excitedly at one of the chickens. "Why, if I had a fine rooster like that, I could get rich with it in the cock-fights."

"Let's go catch it," I suggested.

"No, you stay right here. I'll go catch it all by myself," Kiko said.

My brother stealthily approached the two battling chickens. They were so busy fighting that they didn't notice his approach. When he got near them, he dived and caught one

138

of them by the leg. It struggled and squawked. Kiko was finally able to hold on to both of its wings, and it stood still. I ran over to have a good look at the chicken.

"Kiko, it's a hen," I said.

"What's the matter with you?" my brother asked. "Is the heat making you sick?"

"No, can't you see that it doesn't have a cockscomb or wattles?"

"Who cares about a cockscomb or wattles? Didn't you see it fight?"

"Sure, I saw it fight, but I still say it's a hen."

"A hen! Did you ever see a hen with spurs like these? Or a hen with a tail like this?"

"I don't care about its spurs or tail. I tell you this is a hen. Why, just look at it."

Kiko and I couldn't agree on how to determine the sex of the chicken. If the animal in question had been a water buffalo, then it would have been simple. There would have been no time wasted scrutinizing its tail, hooves, and horns. We would simply have concentrated on one part of the water buffalo's anatomy. We would have looked the water buffalo straight in the face. If it had had a brass ring in its nose, then it would indubitably have been a bull. But chickens are not like water buffalo. So the controversy continued in the fields all morning.

At noon we left to have lunch and argued all the way home. When we arrived at our house, Kiko tied the chicken to a stake. The chicken flapped its wings—and then it crowed!

"There! Did you hear that?" my brother exclaimed triumphantly. "I suppose now you are going to tell me that hens crow and that water buffalo fly."

"It doesn't matter if it crows or not," I said. "That chicken is a hen."

We entered the house and the discussion continued over lunch.

"It is not a hen," Kiko said. "It's a rooster."

"It's a hen," I said.

"It is not."

"It is."

"That's enough," Mother interrupted. "How many times must Father tell you boys not to argue during lunch? What's the argument this time?"

We told Mother and she went out to look at the chicken. "That chicken," she said, "is a rooster that looks just like a hen."

That should have ended the argument. But Father also took a look at the chicken and said: "No, you're wrong. That chicken is a hen that looks just like a rooster."

"Have you been drinking again?" Mother asked.

"No."

"Then what makes you say that this rooster is a hen? Have you ever seen a hen with feathers like that?"

"No, but I've taken care of fighting cocks ever since I was a boy. And you can't tell me that this thing is a rooster."

Before Kiko and I realized what was happening, Mother and Father were arguing about the chicken themselves. Soon Mother was crying. She often started crying when she argued with Father. "You know very well that it's a rooster," she sobbed. "You're just being mean and stubborn. Take another look and see."

"I'm sorry," said Father, "but I know a hen when I see one." Then he hugged her and called her corny names like

141

my madonna and my Maria Clara. He always did that when Mother started crying. Kiko and I felt embarrassed: so we left the house without finishing our meal.

"I know who can settle this question," my brother said.

"Who?" I asked.

"Tenienteng Tasio."

Tenienteng Tasio was the head of the village. I did not think that he was the sort of man who could solve our problem: he was a philosopher. By this I mean that he was a man who explained his strange views with even stranger reasons. For example, he frowned on cockfighting. Now, many people are against cockfighting. They will tell you that it's cruel, or that gambling is bad. But neither of these was the reason be gave. He said that cockfighting was a waste of time. Why? Because it had already been proven that one rooster can beat another.

Tenienteng Tasio did have one factor in his favor though. He was the oldest man in the village. And while this didn't make him a bird expert, still, anything sounds more authoritative if it is said by someone with white hair. So when Kiko suggested that we consult him, I didn't refuse. We decided that we'd accept his decision. Kiko untied the chicken and we took it to Tenienteng Tasio.

"Tenienteng Tasio, is this chicken a male or a female?" Kiko asked.

"That is a question that should concern only another chicken," he replied.

Both Kiko and I were surprised by this answer. But Kiko was stubborn and tried another approach. "Listen, my brother and I happen to have a special interest in this particular chicken. Please give us a clear answer, either yes or no. Is this a rooster?"

"It does not look like any rooster that I have ever seen."

"In that case, it must be a hen," I said.

142

"It does not look like any hen that I have ever seen," was his reply.

My brother and I were dumbfounded. For a long time we remained speechless. Then Tenienteng Tasio asked: "Have you two ever seen an animal like that before?"

Kiko and I had to admit that we hadn't.

"Then how do you know that it's a chicken?" he asked us.

"Well, what else could it be?" Kiko asked in turn.

"It could be another kind of bird."

"Oh, God, no," Kiko said, and we walked away.

"Well, what do we do now?" I asked.

"I know what," my brother said. "Let's go to town and ask Mr. Cruz. He ought to know."

Mr. Eduardo Cruz lived in a nearby town. He had studied poultry husbandry and operated a large egg farm. When we got there, Mr. Cruz was taking his siesta; so Kiko let the chicken run loose in the yard.

The other chickens wouldn't go near ours. Not only did they keep as far away from it as they could, but they didn't even seem to care whether it was a rooster or a hen. Not bothered by this, our chicken chased and disgraced several young hens.

"There, that should prove to you that it's a rooster," exclaimed Kiko.

"It proves nothing of the sort," I said. "It only proves that it has rooster instincts—but it can still be a hen."

As soon as Mr. Cruz was up, we caught the chicken and took it to his office. "Mr. Cruz," Kiko said, "is this a hen or a rooster?"

Mr. Cruz looked at the bird curiously and then said, "Hmm. I don't know. I can't tell right away. I've never come across a chicken that looked like that before."

"Well, is there any way you can find out?"

143

"Why, sure, look at the feathers on its back. If the ends are round, it's a hen; if they're pointed, then it's a rooster."

The three of us examined the chicken's feathers very closely. It had both round and pointed feathers!

"Hmm. Very strange," said Mr. Cruz.

"Is there any other way you could tell?"

"I could kill it and examine its insides."

"No, I don't want it to be killed," said my brother.

I picked up the chicken and we headed back to our village. Kiko was silent most of the way. Then suddenly he snapped his fingers and said: "I know how I can convince you that this is a rooster."

"How?"

"Would you agree that this is a rooster if I put it in a cockfight and it won?"

"If this hen of yours can beat a fighting cock, I'll believe anything," I agreed.

"All right, we'll take it to the cockfights this coming Sunday."

So that Sunday we went to the cockfights. Kiko looked around for an appropriate opponent and finally decided on a red rooster. I recognized the rooster as a famous fighting cock that had once appeared on the cover of the cockfight magazine. It was the rooster that had escaped into the woods once and lured the hens from all the surrounding farms to follow it.

Raising its fine head, the red rooster eyed our chicken arrogantly and shook out its feathers. This scared me, for I knew that when a fighting cock is feeling sexy, it's twice as ferocious.

"Don't make our chicken fight that rooster," I told Kiko. "That's not a Filipino chicken. It's a Texas chicken."

"That doesn't mean anything to me," my brother said. "My rooster will kill it."

"Don't be a fool," I said. "That red cock is a killer. It has killed more chickens than the cholera. There's no rooster in the whole province that can beat it."

My brother wouldn't listen. The match was made and the two birds were made ready to fight. Saber-like spurs were attached to their left legs. I said a secret prayer to Santa Rita de Casia, patroness of the impossible.

Then the fight began. Both birds were released in the center of the cockpit. The Texas rooster scratched the ground as if it was digging a grave for its opponent. Then the two chickens confronted each other. I expected our chicken to die of fright there and then. Instead, a strange thing happened. A love-sick expression came into the red rooster's eyes, and it did a love dance. Naturally this surprised all of us, particularly those who had bet on the red rooster. It became evident that the Texas rooster was infatuated by our chicken. Our chicken took advantage of the red rooster's distraction to attack, thrusting its spurs into the Texas rooster's chest. The fight was over and the referee lifted up our chicken in victory.

"Fixed fight! Unfair!" the crowd shouted.

A riot broke out. People tore the benches apart and used them as clubs. Kiko and I had to escape by the back gate. I held the victorious bird under my arm. We ran toward the grove of palm trees and kept running until we were out of sight of the angry crowd. As soon as we felt safe, we sat down on the ground and rested.

"Now are you convinced that it's a rooster?" Kiko muttered between breaths.

"Yes," I answered.

I was so glad the whole thing was over. But the chicken had other ideas. It began to tremble. Then something warm and round dropped into my hand. The chicken cackled as if it was laughing at us. I looked down and saw an egg!

Illustrated by Solomon Saprid

SRI LANKA

The New Year's Present

by Upali Perera

In Sri Lanka the New Year dawns amid the beating of drums and the bursting of firecrackers, and everyone wears new clothes.

Murie was dressed in a beautiful, brightly colored new dress with flower designs. This year she had received many presents. Her mother and father had given her new clothes and firecrackers, and her aunt had given her a toy train. Of all the presents, she liked the train best. From early that morning she had carried it with her wherever she went.

The sound of the drums and the firecrackers was deafening. Under the tamarind tree near the house, several women were beating the drums. Murie watched their hands move deftly over the surface of the drums. They hit the drums with their palms, with their elbows, and even used their foreheads, always keeping to the right rhythm.

After watching the women for a while, Murie stepped into the compound with the toy train under her arm. She saw Ranjith next door, playing a game with three or four other boys on the verandah. Murie went up to the fence and watched them without making a sound.

Ranjith put some cowries into a coconut shell, held his hand over the top, shook it, and then threw the cowries out onto the ground. Five out of the six turned upside down. "I've got five!" he shouted. Ranjith moved his counter five squares on the game board. The other boys looked very disappointed. Ranjith had already won a kite, five or six mar-

148

bles, and a few firecrackers. And again there were only three
or four squares on the game board before his counter would
reach "home."

"If I can get five again, I'll win this time too," boasted
Ranjith.

Murie felt jealous. She wound up the toy train and put it
on the ground. The train started to move, making a whirring
noise. Hearing the sound, Ranjith turned to see what it was.
Murie wanted to show off her train in front of Ranjith, but
she did not really want to play with him. Murie played with
Ranjith quite often. But ever since she had received the

train, she began to avoid him. Seeing the train, Ranjith ran over toward Murie and threw aside all of his precious winnings.

"Oh, who asked you to come over here? Please go away and leave me alone!" cried Murie when she saw Ranjith coming toward her.

"I want to have a look at your train."

"I won't show it to anyone," said Murie, hugging the train to her chest. Ranjith sat down beside her.

"Didn't I tell you to go away? I'm going to tell my mother on you. Mother! Ranjith is bothering me!" Murie began to shout. Ranjith was frightened and ran home.

Ranjith's father was a poor farmer. Unfortunately, the stream that ran beside their paddy fields had flooded, and their crops were completely destroyed this year. And so they felt the pinch even more during the New Year season when everyone else was getting presents, wearing new clothes, and eating good food. Ranjith and his brother did not even get new clothes this year, let alone toys and firecrackers.

"Murie got lots of presents: new clothes, firecrackers, and

a toy train as well. Oh, what a pretty train that is. And I didn't get anything." Ranjith felt very sad.

Ranjith went back to his house. There was a drain there, paved with cement. Waste water from all the houses in the area flowed along this drain. It never ran dry. Ranjith sat on the edge of the drain and watched the little ripples on the surface of the water. Even though he was watching the ripples, he was seeing Murie's train in his imagination.

The drain became the sea. The cement side of the drain was the railway line. Chug-a-chug, chug-a-chug. That was the sound of the train running along the seashore. "Oh! If only I also had a train, I could drive it along the drain like this. Chug-a-chug, chug-a-chug," Ranjith drove Murie's train in his imagination.

Moss grew at the bottom and along the sides of the drain. A brightly colored piece of paper that came floating along the drain got stuck in the moss. Ranjith bent down and looked at it. It was a beautiful stamp. Then he remembered that Murie collected stamps. Once or twice she had asked him for stamps, but he had none to give her. Upul's stamp album popped into his mind. Upul was Ranjith's brother.

"If I find a few stamps for Murie, she might let me look at her train. She might even let me play with it." This idea came to Ranjith and he ran indoors. Ranjith knew just where Upul kept his stamp album. Upul looked after his album like a miser with gold coins. Upul was flying a kite with his friends in a field. Ranjith could see them far away.

Ranjith went to Upul's desk and opened the drawer slowly. Inside were Upul's books, pens, pencils, marbles, rubber bands, and other things he liked to save. He looked for the album. He came across a spool of string that Upul used for flying his kite. Ranjith left the spool where it was and kept searching for the album. It was at the bottom of the drawer. He took it out quickly and turned the pages.

151

On almost every page in the album, beautiful, brightly colored stamps were pasted. On the first few pages were stamps of Sri Lanka. On the other pages there were foreign stamps. There were stamps with pictures of animals, airplanes, boats, kings and queens.

Ranjith was about to tear a few pages from the album when his mother called from the kitchen. He was very frightened. If he remained silent, his mother would come looking for him. In a panic, he called back: "Yes, Mother?" But he did not move from the spot.

"What are you doing in there? Come here and help me in the kitchen."

"All right, Mother, I'm coming." Ranjith hurriedly tore two or three pages from the stamp album.

"Murie likes foreign stamps, so if I give her still more of these, she might even let me play with the toy train every day," thought Ranjith. He tore out three or four more pages of foreign stamps. He put them aside, left the stamp album in the bottom of the drawer, and arranged the other things on top of it. In his hurry, Ranjith did not put the books back in the right order. The drawer was full and very difficult to close. Taking the pages from the stamp album, he ran to find Murie and show them to her.

"Murie, Murie! Come here and look."

"What is it? Are those stamps?"

"Yes, beautiful stamps. Look, there're a lot of them," said Ranjith standing near the fence.

"Let's see them."

"Should I come over there?" asked Ranjith humbly.

How could she ask him to come over now? She had just chased him away a short time ago. Murie felt ashamed, and at the same time, she felt sorry for him.

"Come on over," said Murie, looking down at the ground.

Ranjith quickly crept through the barbed wire. In his

hurry, he caught his shirt on the barbed wire and tore it. Without taking any notice, he ran toward Murie.

"Where did you get these?"

"I found them," said Ranjith as he handed the stamps to Murie.

"Oh, triangular stamps too!" Murie danced with joy. Ranjith sat down near the train. His hands itched; he wanted so much to touch the train.

"It's all right, you may touch the train. You may even play with it. But I want to keep all these stamps."

Ranjith felt very happy. "Go ahead and keep them. I brought them for you," said Ranjith.

"Then I'll just put them in my room." So saying, Murie

ran inside the house. Ranjith played with the train. Murie soon returned, having left the stamps inside.

"Where did you get this train?" asked Ranjith.

"My aunt brought it for me. That is the box it came in," said Murie, pointing to a cardboard box that had been thrown away. It was a beautiful little cardboard box. On the top and sides were colorful pictures of the train.

"Do you want to keep that?" asked Ranjith.

"It's just an empty box. I threw it away."

"I'll take it then, all right?"

"Take it. I don't mind."

Ranjith picked up the box, opened it, and looked inside. He sniffed the inside of the box. "Oh, what a fine smell," he said.

"That's the smell of the train."

"Let me see," said Ranjith. He picked up the train and sniffed it too.

"It really is the train's smell!" shouted Ranjith.

"Let's play now," suggested Murie.

"We could take the train to the back garden. There's a nice place there to run the train."

"All right, let's go," said Murie, picking up the train.

Ranjith showed Murie the place he had found in the back garden near the drain. Murie started to wind up the train. "Don't wind it, it might fall in the water. Let's just push it along," said Ranjith.

"That's a good idea," replied Murie.

"This is the sea," said Ranjith, keeping the train on the edge of the drain.

"Where is the sea?" asked Murie.

"Here it is, this drain is the sea."

"Oh, you silly, how can this be the sea? It's only a drain."

Ranjith felt ashamed. "Don't tease me, Murie," he pleaded.

"All right, all right, this is the sea. What next?"

"The edge of the drain is the railway line. Now the train is running by the sea. Chug-a-chug, chug-a-chug," Ranjith knelt on the ground and began pushing the train along the edge of the drain.

"Chug-a-chug, chug-a-chug. Now what is that?" asked Murie, laughing.

"Don't laugh. It's the sound of the train running."

"Chug-a-chug is not the sound of a train. Trains go like this: Chugga-chugga-chugga-chugga-toot-toot." Murie used her hand to imitate the wheels of the train going round and round.

Now it was Ranjith's turn to tease Murie. "Look at the funny way you're moving your hand." He laughed.

Murie blushed and looked away. Ranjith was worried that if she got mad, she would take the train away and go home.

"Murie, don't get angry. You're right. That's the sound the train makes: chugga-chugga-chugga-chugga-toot-toot."

Murie looked at Ranjith to see if he meant it.

"There, you're smiling again," said Ranjith. Ranjith started pushing the train along the drain with one hand, and with the other he imitated the wheels just as Murie had done. Murie was pleased.

"Look, we can see the kites that Upul and his friends are flying. One, two, three . . . look how high up that one has gone," said Murie.

Neither of them noticed Upul approaching. "Look here, who gave you permission to count our kites? The kites will probably fall to the ground because of your evil eyes," Upul teased Murie.

"Have you finished flying your kite?" asked Murie.

"Oh, no, that cobra kite is mine. I gave the string to my friend to hold while I get more string from the house. With more string, I can make it fly even higher."

155

"Can I come with you to fly kites?" Murie asked.

"No, your mother would scold all of us. You may come tonight when we send up the lantern kites, though."

"What are lantern kites?" she asked.

"The kite is the same, but we send up a lighted lantern tied to the string. They look like lanterns floating in the night sky."

"Oh, how wonderful! I have some lanterns and candles left over from the festival," Murie said.

"We have lanterns too, but we can use any number of candles. Come tonight. I'd better go now," said Upul and hurried off toward the house.

Ranjith had not said a word. He was frightened when he heard that Upul had gone to get the string. He knew that Upul would discover the missing pages from the stamp album while looking for the string.

"Why do you look so frightened?" Murie asked when she saw the look on Ranjith's face. "Are you scared of your brother?"

"No, it's nothing," said Ranjith and began to play with the train again. After playing for a while, he looked up at Murie and asked: "Did you ask your aunt for this train?"

"No, it's a present from her. I wanted her to give me a doll for my birthday, but this is what I got."

"I don't even have a birthday," said Ranjith.

"How silly! If you don't have a birthday, how were you born?" Murie laughed.

"Then why don't I get presents like other children?"

"Only good children like me get presents," said Murie, patting her chest.

"You have fair skin and so everyone loves you. I am dark; everyone calls me Charcoal and no one loves me. No one ever gives me toys," complained Ranjith. He polished the train with the edge of his shirt.

157

Murie was about to reply when there was a commotion at Ranjith's house. Ranjith was really frightened for he knew his brother had discovered the missing stamps. Ranjith's mother came out of the house. She had Upul's stamp album in her hand and Upul followed behind her.

"Come here, Ranjith!" shouted his mother angrily. "What a terrible thing you've done. Why on earth did you tear those pages from this stamp album?" Ranjith's mother held the album open to show the torn edges of the missing pages.

Ranjith looked down at the ground without a word.

"I asked you to help me in the kitchen, but did you listen? No! This is what you did instead. What a terrible thing to do on New Year's Day!" So saying, she caught Ranjith by the hand, and then she saw the big tear in his shirt. "And what is this? Your shirt is torn! Where have you been creeping around, tell me." Ranjith's mother slapped him on the back and he started crying.

"There's no money in the house to buy new clothes; so I have to sew and darn to keep your old ones together. Do I work so hard just to have you go and rip your shirt? Upul, get me a stick right away," she said.

"Mother, please don't beat me," Ranjith pleaded and held tight to his mother.

Upul rushed and brought a stick from a guava tree.

"Not beat you! I'll teach you a good lesson today!" said his mother and began to beat Ranjith. Ranjith was sobbing and Murie became frightened. She turned away and ran home. After giving Ranjith a good beating, his mother threw the stick aside and went into the house.

Ranjith went and sat crying on the edge of the drain. There were marks on his arms and legs where he had been beaten and he rubbed them sorrowfully.

"Here, chugga-chug." It was Murie's voice. Ranjith turned to look.

"Come here and I'll give you something," she said. Ranjith walked over to her.

"You are a good friend. You never said that you gave the stamps to me even when you were beaten so hard. If my mother had found out, I would have gotten a beating too."

"I never tell on a friend," said Ranjith.

"Take these back and give them to your brother," said

Murie, showing Ranjith the stamps she had been keeping behind her back.

"I don't have to give them back. I've already had a beating for them. You may keep them."

"Only bad children steal. I didn't know these stamps were stolen. I thought they were yours."

"Yes, I am bad. I steal. So what?" replied Ranjith stubbornly.

"You are very bad. Take these and give them back right now. Then your mother and Upul won't be angry any more," persisted Murie.

"I won't."

"Then I won't let you play with my train any more." Murie held the train out toward Ranjith.

"It's all right. I have its empty cardboard box. I'll play with that."

"If I give you the train to keep, will you take the stamps and give them back to your brother?"

"Could I really have it forever?" asked Ranjith. "What if your mother finds out?"

"I've already asked her and she said that since it was a present for me, I can do anything I want with it."

"Is it really true?" Ranjith stretched out his hands to take the train.

"But you must promise to give these stamps to your brother," said Murie.

"All right, I promise." Ranjith took the stamps and the toy train in both hands. Then off he ran toward the house calling his mother.

Translated by H. H. Kumarapperuma
Illustrated by Somasiri Herath

THAILAND

Little Noi's Whale

by Wiriya Sirisingh

Little Noi would be returning to Bangkok on the following day. She would have only one more day to stay with us; so we planned to go to the sea again. This time we would go fishing.

"I like fishing very much, Lek," Little Noi told me eagerly. "I'll catch the largest fish in the whole world."

"Oh, come on, Little Noi," I said. "Do you think you can force the fish to swallow the bait? Why do you think you'll catch such a big fish?"

"Why not? We'll fish in the deep blue sea, won't we? Fish there are all really big, right?"

That was a reasonable answer, I thought. I should have kept quiet.

On our trip to the sea, there were four of us. Besides Little Noi, Squid, and me, we also had Tue, Little Noi's nursemaid. At first we thought we would ask one of the servants from our house to sail the boat, but everyone was busy, and in the end I did the sailing by myself. Squid was in charge of preparing lines, hooks, bait, and things like that. Tue would make sure that we had enough to eat during the trip.

With a pair of pliers, Squid cut pieces of wire about seven inches long from a large coil. Then, to both ends of each of the short wires he tied a hook. At the middle of each wire he attached a plastic line.

"No rods?" Little Noi asked, a little surprised.

"We won't need them. We can hold the line in our hands. When a fish takes the bait we can pull the line up. That's all."

"I don't like it," complained Little Noi. "We don't even have any weights."

"That piece of wire is heavy enough, Little Noi," Squid explained. "When we drop the wire, it will sink down to the bottom of the sea with those hooks. This way of fishing is really good, you know. You can catch two fish at a time."

"Really?" she asked. She could not quite believe it.

"Certainly. See, there's a hook on each end of the wire."

Squid provided each of us with a set of the homemade fishing gear. When everything was ready, we stepped down into the boat, carrying all of the things that we planned to use during the trip.

Our boat was a middle-sized one, with a roof in the center. It was usually used for delivering sugar, oil, rice, and those kinds of things to customers on both sides of the canal. I sailed the boat slowly along the canal and out to sea. At last we were so far from land that we could not see the houses along the canal anymore. What we saw now was only the sea and the sky. A flock of white sea birds were hovering over the surface of the water, looking for fish. Some perched on the fishing stakes. They looked absolutely white. When our boat approached them, they all flew away, up into the sky.

"Don't you dare allow our boat to get stranded, Lek," Tue teased me joyfully. I assured her that I would not. "How do you know where the channel is, Lek?" she continued.

"You can tell from those big waves, Tue." Squid, who was sitting next to her, explained: "If the boat is sailing in the deep channel, the waves will be horizontal to the boat, but if it is not in the channel, or if it is in the shallow part of the channel, the waves will hit the boat head on."

"Is the sea deep here?" Little Noi wanted to know.

"No, when it gets late, it will completely dry up here."

I sailed on until we came to a suitable location for fishing. Then I turned the engine off and walked to the prow. Squid and I pushed a pole into the sea to measure the depth. It soon hit the sea floor and we knew that this part of the sea

was not very deep. Its depth was equal only to the height of the two of us put together. After the pole was fixed tightly in the sea floor, I tied the boat to it so that we would not float away from our location.

"Are there any fish down there?" Little Noi asked.

"Oh, plenty," I said. "You can choose any place on this boat to fish from."

We used shrimps for bait. We carefully hid the hooks inside the shrimps so that the fish would not see them. Then we dropped our lines to the bottom of the shallow sea. Little Noi stood at the prow of the boat. Tue was at the other end of the boat, while Squid and I stood on each side.

"Should we have a contest?" Little Noi asked. "The one who catches the most fish will be the winner. Oh, oh, my line is jerking!" she screamed with excitement. "The fish here are so greedy."

"Let's see who can catch the largest fish; then he or she

165

will be the winner." Squid proposed this new idea and we all agreed.

"I got one," Tue cried loudly and quickly pulled her line in. A tiny fish was struggling helplessly on the hook. "Oh, how tiny you are," she murmured and threw the fish back into the sea.

"Wait. Oh, no. Why did you do that, Tue?" Squid objected. "How can you call this fishing?"

"It was too small, boy. I'll catch a bigger one. Don't you worry about it," said Tue as she prepared to try again. She dropped the hooks into the water again with new shrimps carefully attached.

"Mine has been jerking for a long time. Can I draw the line up now?" said Little Noi.

"Silly girl. I bet only the bare hooks are left," I cried out hopelessly. "Draw the line up right now."

By the time we finally drew Little Noi's line into the boat, the bait was all gone. "Next time, when you feel that jerking, pull the line up sharply," I told her. "Then the hooks will catch in the fish's mouth."

"Is that so?" Little Noi seemed to be learning how to fish for the first time in her life. "Next time I'll catch two fish at once."

There were many fish in the sea at that time of day. Not too long afterward, Squid and I had caught three or four fish each. But the only fish we could catch was that tiny kind that Tue had caught before. It was a little smaller than a small tuna and had many scales. Its head was small, but its mouth was large and funny-looking. It tasted very good and didn't have many bones. Some fishermen even lived by catching just this kind of fish. They had to catch at least a hundred a day, but they were one of the best sellers on the market.

"I've got a big one!" Little Noi suddenly screamed with

166

excitement. All three of us dropped our lines and surrounded her. Her line pulled tight. Something was pulling on it very hard.

"I'll be the winner," said Little Noi. "What should I do now?" She looked around to us for help. She could not make up her mind what to do next. If she pulled it too hard, the thin plastic line would break. But if she did not pull the line in, the fish would pull it down until it ran out and the line would break anyway.

"Give it to me, Little Noi," Squid volunteered.

"Yes, please help me," she said, and quickly gave the line to him.

Squid carefully, gradually, pulled the line up toward the boat. If the fish pulled too hard on the line, Squid stopped pulling for a while. Then he would begin to pull again. He started and stopped over and over again. The rest of us waited impatiently. We wanted to know what kind of stupid fish would have swallowed Little Noi's hook.

"I'm sure it's a whale." Little Noi was more anxious than any of the rest of us. She walked back and forth impatiently, her arms folded tightly in excitement.

"Are you crazy? How can you catch a whale here?" said Tue. "Whales live in the ocean. There aren't any whales here."

"You are really out of date, Tue," said Little Noi, for she was sure she knew more than her nursemaid. "Not long ago, a newspaper said that a dead whale was found on a beach near here. You read about it, didn't you?"

"And if that one was dead, which one could be eating your bait right now?" Tue still disagreed with Little Noi, but her voice was a little less sure than in the beginning.

And then the most exciting moment finally came. Squid succeeded in pulling in the line and the hooks and all. But what was caught on Little Noi's line was not a whale or even one of those tiny fish. It was only a very large old basket.

"Here it is, Little Noi's whale!" we all shouted.

Translated by Lamoon Ruttakorn
Illustrated by Tream Chachumporn

VIET NAM

An Elephant Named Storm

by Vu Hung

Editors' Note.   This is the first episode of a much longer story. Hence its ending has been slightly modified for purposes of plot unity.

It was a summer day almost forty years ago. The sun was beating down on the jungle. Complete silence, not a breath of wind. The trees stood motionless. The air was stifling, heated to a white haze.

Toward late afternoon, the heat became almost unbearable. People stayed at home instead of going out to work in

the terraced fields. Chickens and dogs stood breathlessly in the yard, overcome by the heat.

Rem, an old Kha tribesman, was squatting on the floor, gazing out of the door at the sky. His forehead was wrinkled in thought.

"Heavens!" he groaned. "Big storm coming."

In the animal park the elephants were getting restless. They swayed wearily, chained to stakes sunk deep in the ground. From time to time they jerked their trunks into the air as if to gulp down more air and bellowed nervously.

"Just listen to those elephants," the old man muttered to himself. "Bet it'll rain hard." He stood up, took an elephant goad down from the wall, and went down the ladder to the ground.

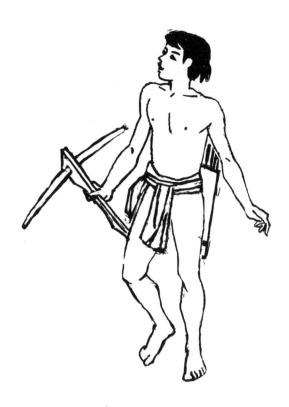

"Dik," he called. "Hey, Dik!"

There was a long hoot from the jungle.

"Dik!" the old man shouted again, waving the goad toward the jungle. "Come here."

A boy emerged from the bush, a crossbow in his hand, a quiver dangling from his waist. His brown chest was glistening with sweat.

"I must go now," Dik said to his companion, looking back regretfully at the place where he had spent half the day with Srung, waiting beneath a squirrel hole.

"Be quiet!" Srung's brown face peered out from the bush. "If you make noise, the squirrels won't come."

"Grandfather called for me. I have to go now."

"All right. I'll bring you a squirrel to make soup with tonight."

"I won't make soup," said Dik, smiling. "I'll make some roast squirrel for grandfather to eat with his rice wine." Winking at his friend, Dik darted off toward the house. Beads of sweat stood out on his glowing face.

He rushed up the ironwood ladder, worn to a silky smoothness by time and use. Old Rem took the crossbow and quiver from him and handed him the goad.

"Go fetch Lekdam."

"Why don't you let him enjoy a good shower?"

"It's not a shower. Storm's coming."

Dik hurried down the ladder, two rungs at a time. Then, flourishing the goad like a professional mahout, he raced off to the elephant park.

As soon as he got there, he unchained Lekdam. The old elephant showed his appreciation by caressing the boy's face with the tip of his trunk and rubbing the boy's sides with his tusks. Then, with infinite care, he wound his trunk around the boy's waist, lifted him up, and placed Dik gently on his broad back. Dik straddled the huge animal and prodded his neck with the goad.

"Go! Go!" he ordered, assuming the tone of a grown-up.

At a stately pace, Lekdam started off, dragging along a length of chain.

By that time other people were coming to take their elephants home. The village became unusually lively. Elephants were trumpeting. Children were running madly about, throwing their arms in the air as if they were trying to embrace the rising wind.

The wind was gathering strength, becoming stronger and stronger with each gust. The elephant park was deserted now; only the dry grass blew. Birds were fighting the wind, desperately trying to get home before the storm broke. The sky darkened. Suddenly clouds were ripped by lightning. Hardly had the children reached shelter when the storm

173

broke, spilling great torrents of rain on the bamboo roofs. Trees swayed drunkenly in the wind, their leaves falling in great quantities.

The floorboards of Old Rem's house, secured though they were by sturdy ironwood pillars, were heaving and shaking as though they would jerk loose at any moment.

Old Rem raked the fire and the flames leaped up, throwing his and his grandson's shadows onto the wall. Thunder crashed somewhere high in the mountains. It was so loud that it sounded as though it were right above them. Then there was a prolonged rumbling coming from the mountains.

"Landslide," the old man whispered.

Straining their ears, they could hear rocks falling, trees crashing, and wild animals howling in fear.

"Landslide," Old Rem repeated, awed by the ruthless strength of nature.

He and the boy crept over to the window and looked out. There was a blinding flash of lightning followed immediately by another deafening crash of thunder. In that brief flash, they saw something like a wide road running down the mountain slope, and they could make out boulders hurtling down the path. Amid this orgy of unearthly sounds, they could hear the braying of frightened elephants.

"Wild elephants," remarked Dik in a whisper.

"Yes, wild elephants," agreed the old man, listening carefully.

This was not unusual in their village. At the beginning of the rainy season, when young plants were sprouting everywhere on mountain slopes and in fields, wild elephants would come down from the mountains for food. They moved around all the time, going wherever it was raining. This had been their custom from time immemorial.

From below the house, the old elephant Lekdam was beating his trunk against the floor. The other elephants in the

174

neighborhood were also stamping impatiently. Then they started trumpeting and pulling at their chains.

From somewhere at the farthest end of the village a gong sounded, and soon gongs were heard everywhere, their metallic reverberations drowning the wail of the wind. People all over the village were signaling the presence of wild animals. Everyone was on the alert.

A herd of wild elephants was approaching. Their high-pitched cries had an undeniably ferocious quality. Soon they came into sight, huge black shapes in the gloom. The whole village shook with the force of their stamping. But they disappeared quite soon and the stamping was lost in the howling wind.

Long afterwards, the old man and Dik heard one lone elephant heading for the village. Its heavy feet made loud splashes in the pools of water made by the storm. The elephant paused every now and then as if it was lost.

Old Rem and Dik could see it now.

"A stray elephant!" the old man exclaimed with great excitement. Then, as agile as a squirrel, he made a leap to the gong hanging on the wall. He waited until the elephant had reached the village clearing, then gave a quick succession of blows on the gong.

Without being told, Dik threw open the door and grabbed the coil of buffalo-hide rope. Rain lashed furiously in their faces. Dik jumped down onto the ground, went up to Lekdam, and unchained him. As Lekdam was rising up on his knees with Dik perched on his back, the old man dropped down onto the elephant's neck with the huge coil of rope. He took his seat in front, his knees pressed against the backs of the elephant's ears. He held a long pole in his hands. A sliding noose hung from the far end of the pole and was connected to the coil of rope.

Old Rem's signal had been heard throughout the village.

175

Now people were beating their gongs in answer and elephants were being taken out.

Excited by the rain and all the activity, Lekdam set out at a gallop toward the village gate. Lekdam's trunk was raised high in the air. He was gaining fast on the stray elephant. Sensing danger, the stray elephant trundled off as fast as he could, limping on one hind leg. He must have been wounded during the landslide. Although he was a calf elephant, he was almost as big as a full-grown male. At one point when he turned back to look at his pursuers, Dik had a glimpse of a pair of tusks beginning to grow.

"What an elephant!" the boy exclaimed in wonder.

Old Rem slapped hard on Lekdam's neck, urging him on. Lekdam started to close in on the other elephant. There was

a flash of lightning, and by its light Old Rem was able to get one of the elephant's hind legs in his noose.

"Play out the rope," he shouted to Dik as he dropped to the ground. Dik fumbled with the coil, but finally managed to slide it off Lekdam's back.

Meanwhile, the calf continued to run, taking up the slack. The old man let out more rope and secured the end to a tree.

The stray elephant suddenly stopped short. He tried to free himself, making the taut rope vibrate. Old Rem, having driven a stake into the ground to strengthen the rope, regained his place on Lekdam's neck.

Old Rem ordered Lekdam to approach the stray. The calf cowered, crying out for rescue. He also attempted to defend himself, but gave up the idea and began to retreat. The older

elephant, probably moved by the calf's terror, patted the calf's back consolingly with his trunk. Then moving forward quickly, he pushed the calf against a big tree and, flinging out his massive trunk, took hold of the trunk of the young elephant.

A couple of other mahouts rushed up with their elephants to help. They made all sorts of noises, both threatening and reassuring, while circling the wild elephant. Then, with more ropes, they tied the captive fast to the tree. When Lekdam finally released his hold on the calf, it was near midnight and the storm was almost over.

Back at home, Old Rem fed more wood to the dying fire and sat down again beside it with his grandson. He rolled himself a big cigar, lighted it, took a long puff, and let the smoke out luxuriously.

Rem had worked and worked for years before he managed to acquire an elephant of his own. That was when he was young. He followed the hunters in their yearly journeys to the western side of the mountains. A couple of elephants were the most a hunting season would yield, and there were always more hunters than elephants to share out. So priority was given to the seniors, and Rem had to wait for eight years before his turn came.

When he was given to Rem, Lekdam was already past his prime, but he was still all muscle. And thanks to Lekdam, Rem's family fared much better. Rem and his son, Dik's father, used to take the elephant to the mountains to clear land for cultivation or to haul timber. He was also used to carry salt and other commodities to Laos or to remote villages in the southern highlands.

Now Lekdam was old. Like his master, he could not be of much use. It had been the wish of Old Rem's son, who with his young wife had died in an epidemic, that Dik be

given a new elephant to take the place of the aging Lekdam.

This request had kept Old Rem sleepless for many a night. He blamed himself for his failure to provide property for his only grandson. What would happen to the boy if all he inherited was an aging elephant? The stray calf, therefore, seemed to be a miraculous piece of luck. The old man, dreaming of his grandson's happiness and prosperity, yearned to feast his eyes on the new elephant. He wanted to tame the animal as quickly as possible.

As for Dik, he was speechless with joy. His mind was racing: Lekdam is old now. It's time to retire him. He's worked so many years for Grandfather. He will be too old in five or six years. Grandfather should turn him loose into the jungle. His place will be taken by the young elephant. Dik felt as though he were dreaming, but the contrary was proved by the constant trumpeting of the stray elephant, to which he listened with great satisfaction.

The wind, which had been hissing through the many cracks in the wall, was dying down. An occasional flash of lightning or a roll of thunder in the distance was the only reminder of the great storm the evening before. Somewhere at the edge of the jungle, early birds were already twittering.

The birds put an end to the old man's musings. "I had to work hard for eight years before I could have an elephant," he told the boy, giving him a warm smile. "Now a calf elephant has come to us. It's like discovering a treasure. So what about calling him Treasure? He's yours to keep and I want to give him a really beautiful name."

"Treasure," the boy thought out loud. "But the elephant is more than just a treasure, Grandfather. I want a better, a stronger name."

They both thought in silence for some time. Suddenly Dik clapped his hands. "I've got it!" he cried. "This elephant came to us in a storm, and he's sure to grow up to be as strong and brave as a storm. So that's what we'll call him — Storm, my beautiful, strong, brave Storm."

Old Rem smiled and nodded his head. "Storm," he repeated smiling.

Then, filled with a sudden rush of gratitude, the boy knelt on the floor in front of his grandfather and embraced the old man's legs. Amost in unison, as though calling out to the new elephant, once more they both—grandfather and grandson—said: "Storm."

Translated by Ngoai Van
Illustrated by Vu Huyen

The Contributors

BANGLADESH

Syed Shamsul Hoque is a popular poet, novelist, and short-story writer. He has also worked extensively with radio and film and is now working on various cultural programs for television.

Hashem Khan's illustrations have appeared in hundreds of books and magazines. He is a lecturer at the Bangladesh College of Arts and Crafts in Dacca.

BURMA

Gayetni (U Ye Myint) has published numerous articles, stories, and novels. He is now associated with the Ministry of Information.

Myo Win is a commercial artist who has received many prizes and has studied ancient Burmese art.

CHINA

Xiao Ping has published several collections of short stories in China. He is presently Dean of the Chinese Literature Department at a teachers' college in Shandong.

Zhou Si-cong, who specializes in Chinese-style figure painting, has exhibited her work widely. She is presently working at the Beijing Academy of Chinese Painting.

INDIA

Margaret R. Bhatty is a free-lance writer who has been widely published in India and abroad. She is currently working on several novels.

Yusuf Lien is a self-taught artist of many talents, having worked over the years on book illustration, comic strips, Islamic calligraphy, portraits, and wildlife.

181

INDONESIA

Moh. Ambri was a teacher, editor, and writer. Before his death in 1936, he published about twenty novels, short stories, translations, and adaptions.

Syahwil has worked as a painter, illustrator, and writer. His works have been exhibited all over the world.

IRAN

Nader Ebrahimi is a well-known Iranian writer.

Parviz Kalantari's paintings have been exhibited widely.

JAPAN

Kenji Miyazawa was a poet and author of children's stories who specialized in stories about farmers.

Osamu Tsukasa is a self-taught artist whose original style is found in many picture books and illustrations.

KOREA

O Yong-su was an award-winning author who edited a literary magazine.

Kim Young-ju is a Western-style painter whose works have been widely exhibited.

MALAYSIA

Ali Majid is a tutor at the University of Malaysia who has also worked as an editor and has written short stories, poems, plays, and essays.

Ariff Mohamad has worked in cloth hand printing and is now an artist at the Dewan Bahasa dan Pustaka.

NEPAL

Ramesh Bikal has published many novels, short stories, and essays. He also works in radio and magazines and is now with the Nepalese Ministry of Education.

Tek Bir Mukhiya is a self-taught artist and chief designer for the Nepal Association of Fine Arts.

PAKISTAN

Mahmud Khawar is a prolific writer and publisher of novels and children's stories. He is now working on a children's encyclopedia and edits a general story magazine.

Mohammad Wasim is an artist and cartoonist.

PHILIPPINES

Alejandro R. Roces is the former secretary of the Republic of the Philippines and former chairman of the Unesco National Commission of the Philippines.

Solomon Saprid is a Filipino artist whose monuments grace the city of Manila. He has won national as well as international awards.

SRI LANKA

Upali Perera is a journalist, translator, and story writer who specializes in children's and feature writing. He is with the editorial staff of a leading weekly in Colombo.

Somasiri Herath's art work has been exhibited many times. He is now active as a book designer.

THAILAND

Wiriya Sirisingh is a free-lance writer, newspaper columnist, and children's book publisher.

Tream Chachumporn is a leading artist who specializes in comics and illustration of children's books and magazines.

VIET NAM

Vu Hung works in the Hanoi Foreign Languages Publishing House and specializes in children's literature.

Vu Huyen specialized in silk painting and wood engraving at the Hanoi Fine Arts College and is now a staff member of the Hanoi Foreign Languages Publishing House.

RENNER LEARNING RESOURCE CENTER
ELGIN COMMUNITY COLLEGE
ELGIN ILLINOIS 60120

The "weathermark" identifies this book as a production of John Weatherhill, Inc., publishers of fine books on Asia and the Pacific. Supervising editor: Meredith Weatherby. Typography and layout of illustrations: Miriam F. Yamaguchi. Composition: Kenkyusha Printing Company, Tokyo. Engraving of plates and printing: Inshokan Printing Company, Tokyo. Binding: Wada Binderies, Tokyo. The typeface used is Monotype Baskerville.